THE IRANIAN PUZZLE PIECE

Understanding Iran in the Global Context

MARINE CORPS UNIVERSITY
QUANTICO, VIRGINIA
2009

Edited by Amin Tarzi

Note on Transliteration

In this work, an attempt has been made to simplify transliteration of non-Latin terms and names. As such, the system does not strictly follow any of the standard transliteration systems commonly in use in academic works in the United States. With exception of some proper names, the use of diacritical marks has been limited to few cases. Moreover, in this work, the Arabic and Persian consonant is not transliterated; however, the vowel that is attached to the consenant has been represented by that vowel. For example, Ali, not 'Ali; or Masud, not Mas'ud. When terms of Arabic origin are used in reference of Iran, the Persian transliteration has been adopted, such as mojahedin, not mujahidin; or sayyed, not sayyid.

Terms and names which have become Anglicized in major dictionaries of the English language, such as "Quran," are not transliterated. Likewise, terms such as "mullah" are used in place of "mulla." Names which have common usage but are not transliterated are used in their familiarized form, such as Saddam Hussein.

Published by Books Express Publishing
Copyright © Books Express, 2010
ISBN 978-1-780391-40-3

Books Express publications are available from all good retail and online booksellers. For publishing proposals and direct ordering please contact us at: info@books-express.com

Contents

Illustrations

Iran

International boundary
Province *(ostān)* boundary
★ National capital
● Province *(ostān)* capital
Railroad
Road

0   250 Kilometers
0   250 Miles

Lambert Conformal Conic Projection, SP 12/0/36N

Foreword

Major General (Ret) Donald R. Gardner

This book contains the collected work from "The Iranian Puzzle Piece: Understanding Iran in the Global Context." This one-day international symposium, held at Marine Corps University (MCU), was cohosted by MCU and the Marine Corps University Foundation and was coordinated by the Marine Corps University's Middle East Studies (MES) that was established in 2007.

MCU is a world-class educational institution focused on the art and science of war and is fully engaged in and dedicated to its students' professional military education. Through educational forums like the "Iranian Puzzle Piece," MCU develops the professional competence of Marines and other leaders. Knowledge can be a powerful weapon for the 21st-century Marine. It was under this prerogative that MCU initiated the MES to help educate and prepare the next generation of leaders and war-fighters for the missions ahead.

The purpose of MES is to broaden the understanding of the Middle East and to assess emerging issues in the region that affect the Department of Defense, specifically the Marine Corps. The MES focused its initial efforts on Iran, providing a balanced assessment of Iran in terms of all diplomatic, information, military, and economic areas of influence. The MES supports the University and the Marine Corps by conducting lectures, seminars, and briefings on Iran and its foreign policy.

The symposium from which these essays originated offered a forum to enhance the overall understanding of Iran, exploring its internal dynamics, regional perspectives, and extra-regional factors and examining its near-term political and strategic options and their potential impact on the United States and the Marine Corps. This event joined together colleagues from the Armed Services, joint, interagency, coalition partners, and security communities and explored various perspectives to help develop an understanding of the role played by the Islamic Republic of Iran in the global community.

I would sincerely like to thank our distinguished authors and speakers whose expertise and insight made the "Iranian Puzzle Piece" an absolute success and this timely publication possible.

Donald R. Gardner
Major General, U.S. Marine Corps (Retired)
President Emeritus, Marine Corps University

Introduction
Amin Tarzi

The legendary period of Persian history begins far back in the mists of time. It is the custom to assume that legend means fiction; but historians are now beginning to perceive that the legends of a nation are often not only more interesting and poetic than what is called its authentic history, but that they really suggest actual facts, while nothing can be more fascinating than the study of such legends. No country has more attractive legends than Persia; and to judge from them we cannot avoid the conclusion that no nation now existing has such a continuous vitality as the old land of Cyrus and Xerxes.

Samuel G. W. Benjamin
First U.S. Minister to Persia[1]

The Islamic Republic of Iran, birthed from the legendary Persian Empire, remains the complex blend of fact and narrative described by Benjamin in 1902. It is this complexity that shapes Iranian national identity, policies, and strategies and defines its relations with others. The web of fact and fiction; history and legend; reality and perception bodes well for poetry, but it presents a challenge for political decision making in an international arena where waters are already muddied. A symposium at Marine Corps University, "The Iranian Puzzle Piece: Understanding Iran in the Global Context," held in September 2008, sought to clarify the waters o examine the "puzzle piece" labeled Iran and understand how it fits into the larger, global puzzle. Out of that symposium came these papers, which provide insight into the multifaceted nature of Iran and its regime, examine the feasibility and possible outcomes of official engagement of the regime, and discuss the domestic, regional, and international implications of Iran's nuclear ambitions.

---

1. Samuel G. W. Benjamin, *The Story of Persia* (New York: G.P. Putnam's Sons, 1902), 1.

1

It is the pursuit of nuclear technology that has catapulted Iran to center stage. Escalated tensions in the region as well as internationally have prompted calls for engagement and, at the same time, stern warnings and sanctions. How the game plays out determines if this becomes a potential conflict flashpoint or if Iran becomes a responsible, transforming partner in the region and beyond. To ensure the latter instead of the former requires a deep understanding of Iran's power structures and the grievances that thwart rapprochement to determine with whom and about what to speak, a thorough analysis of the Iran's nuclear posture to avoid premature detonation of this explosive issue, and an appreciation for Iran's potential in the region to influence its choices to positive ends.

With Whom to Talk?

In his chapter on dialogue between the United States and Iran, Karim Sadjadpour argues the futility of the isolationist position but recognizes the challenges facing the United States in discerning with whom or which center of power to engage. The overlapping and complicated power structure of the Islamic Republic was intentionally designed in 1979 to obfuscate lines of authority and ensure no single entity became powerful enough to bend to foreign pressure, resulting in a myriad of power centers, none with supreme authority. While decision-making processes remain ambiguous, both Sadjadpour and Mohsen M. Milani, in his chapter on Iran's policy toward Iraq, maintain that the Supreme Leader Ayatollah Sayyed Ali Hoseyni Khamenei has the most power within the Iranian political structure; however, both note that he may not act in isolation like Iran's last monarch, Mohammad Reza Shah Pahlavi, whose reign ended with the Islamic Revolution in 1979.

Khamenei's role in the controversial presidential election held on 12 June 2009 has further complicated this discussion. The election pitted three candidates against the incumbent, Mahmud Ahmadinejad. Other candidates included Mir-Hoseyn Musavi, a former prime minister; Mohsen Rezaei, a former commander of the Islamic Revolution Guard Corps; and Mehdi Karrubi, former speaker of the Iranian parliament

(*Majles*). Preelection predictions were that if Khamenei stayed neutral and did not intervene on behalf of his protégé Ahmadinejad, Musavi would win. However, as pointed out by Ali M. Ansari in his chapter on Ahmadinejad, Khamenei's preelection support of Ahmadinejad's policies and presidency revealed his political leanings. Sadjadpour's prediction that Khamenei would heavily influence the electoral outcome materialized as the events of June 2009 unfolded.

By placing his office and his person on the side of Ahmadinejad rather than acting as an impartial judge in the controversial elections, Khamenei has bogged down the office of the supreme leader with political minutia and raised further questions about his objectivity and apolitical position. Khamenei's backing of Ahmadinejad is not new, and as Ansari explains, does not have its roots in ideology but rather in an attempt to consolidate power within the Iranian power structure. Khamenei has been seen to largely endorse Ahmadinejad's first-term governmental reforms and his policies, even as other conservatives and a large number of Iranians find themselves farther apart from Ahmadinejad's policies and ideological worldview. For Khamenei, this partnership may prove costly. He has alienated a large number of his peers and traditional supporters, and his ability to make tough decisions on Iran's foreign relations and policies is being called into question. This short-term victory may have long-term negative effects on his or his office's position of supremacy in Iran's decision-making process. Khamenei did not follow Milani's advice to remain neutral in the electoral process so that his position would be secure. So now the questions remain: is Khamenei the person with whom the U.S. should engage, or has the pendulum of power begun to swing?

What Should the Parties Discuss?

If or when negotiations between the United States and Iran occur, determining the agenda will be a tricky endeavor. Ronald E. Neumann cautions, in his chapter on U.S.-Iranian negotiations, that it is important to keep in mind the almost irreconcilable positions of the parties. One country's desired outcome is anathema to the other. While the commonalities are few, the list of grievances, both historical and current, is long, the latest entry being the accusations made by the Iranian regime against a number of Western countries for alleged involvement in the post-election protests and demonstrations. Neumann recounts the myriad of hurdles—historical misunderstandings, suspicion, legal battles, and internal domestic opposition—that both parties will face and have to overcome on the path to rapprochement. While daunting, Neumann sees value in pursuing negotiations, if only to chip away at the hardened positions to slowly improve relations.

There are many deal breakers for both Iran and the United States. Three of the most intractable are Iran's rejection of Israel's right to exist; its support for terrorism; and of course the nuclear issue. Neumann describes Iran's nuclear posture and its continued support of terrorism as the major issues, adding that there are numerous other issues as potentially intractable. Sadjadpour lists Iran's position on Israel as the greatest obstacle to improved relations, as he notes belligerency toward Israel is one of three ideological symbols of the Islamic Republic, and he sees the nuclear and Israeli issues as inextricably linked. Gerald M. Steinberg, in his chapter on Iran in the Israeli threat perception, explains Iran's support for Hezbollah and Hamas and its nuclear ambitions as manifestations of the existential threat Israel continues to face from the Iranian regime. This threat has been in existence since the 1979 Islamic Revolution and is perceived to be escalating with the rise of Iran's nuclear ambitions. He cautions that Israel is considering all options to counter this threat.

Khamenei illustrated his distaste for any hint of niceties toward Israel in his public rebuking of Ahmadinejad in July 2009, this just shortly after having backed him in the elections. As part of his new government, Ahmadinejad appointed his son's father-in-law, Esfandiar Rahim Mashaii, as his first vice president. The first vice president wields a degree of power within Iran's power structure, leading cabinet sessions in the absence of the president. Khamenei, however, issued a decree ordering Ahmadinejad to remove Mashaii from his post and asserting he has no place in the current cabinet.[2] According to *Tehran Times*, in 2008 while serving as director of Iran's Cultural Heritage, Tourism and Handicrafts Organization, Mashaii had said, "Iran is a friend of the Israeli people," which violated the official Iranian position on the "Zionist regime"—the name by which Iran refers to Israel.[3] This simple remark about friendship between peoples could not be tolerated by Khamenei and those around him, as it is seen as legitimizing Israel.

That said, there may be an opportunity for Iran to revisit its stance on Israel if it is determined to be expedient to the regime. Milani discusses Iran's use of *maslehat* (expediency) as a tool to weigh the costs and benefits of potential actions and provides examples of how *maslehat* has been employed in recent history to ensure the regime's objectives are fulfilled. Sadjadpour believes that the regime may change its position regarding the legitimacy of the Israeli state if the Palestinians reach an agreed path forward, which the regime could justify by invoking *maslehat*.

Iran's Nuclear Program

Despite Iranian assurances otherwise, the international community believes Iran is in pursuit of a nuclear weapons capability. Simon Shercliff, in his chapter on the Iranian nuclear issue, explains that this is a result of the huge mistrust of Iranian intentions and motivations and a complete disconnect between Iranian civilian needs and technological pursuits. And despite U.S. assurances that the U.S. does not seek regime change, Iran is convinced otherwise. So suspicion is alive and well on all fronts. Shercliff asserts, however, that regardless of Iran's stated motivations, intentions, and claims of scientific progress, the international community is right to be concerned about Iran's nuclear activities. Sadjadpour contends that resolution of this issue will first require the United States and Iran to settle broader diplomatic

---

2. "Leader Has Ordered President to Dismiss Rahim-Mashaii: Top MP," *Tehran Times*, 22 July 2009 (http:www.tehrantimes.com/NCms/2007.asp?code=199282).
   3. Ibid.

challenges, which as stated above will prove challenging and require profound and mature diplomacy on both sides.

Sadjadpour points out that the devil is in the details. The most significant detail is that of time. Once the nuclear cat is out of the bag, paradigms shift, and there is no turning back. Time is influencing the direction of both the existing multilateral diplomatic approach regarding Iran's nuclear program—E3+3, comprised of China, France, Germany, Russia, the United Kingdom, and the United States—and other potential advocates of Iran changing its course. As such, Shercliff advocates for forcing Iran's hand, compelling Iran to choose between cooperation and confrontation before it is too late. Neumann promotes a two-pronged approach, borrowing former Israeli Prime Minister Yitzhak Rabin's strategy of negotiating as if there is no fighting and fighting as if there are no talks. Neither talks nor pressures should restrict the employment of the other, as a balance between the two ensures a more successful outcome.

Steinberg affirms Neumann's recommended approach, noting that Israel's policy is to consider all available options to resolve Iran's nuclear issue while pursuing a diplomatic solution. However, in the end, as time pressures build, patience for a lengthy diplomatic process may wane, or the process will be overcome by events. Steinberg, in closing, provides an ominous yet realistic assessment of Israeli perceptions vis-à-vis Iran's threat:

> Overall, the Iranian nuclear threat has reinforced the realism that forms the Israeli approach to security threats. While there is still hope that international action, including serious sanctions, will stop Iran before the nuclear finish line, this is by no means assured. Proposals by foreign diplomats and academics suggesting that alliances such as North Atlantic Treaty Organization (NATO) membership for Israel could provide a sufficient response to an Iranian nuclear capability, or that a defense treaty with the United States would be important in this respect, are not likely to be seen as effective by Israelis.

The U.S. is seen as weakened economically and overcommitted in Iraq and Afghanistan, and the weakness of European members of NATO, particularly with respect to security, reinforces the skepticism. While there are many complexities, the possibility for a preventive Israeli military strike remains significant.

Ali-Akbar Salehi, the newly appointed director of the Atomic Energy Organization of Iran, called for closure of his country's nuclear dossier on 19 July 2009, citing completion of all required legal and technical discussions and noting that any remaining concerns are undocumented and unsubstantiated.[4] If Salehi's actions are indicative of what Ahmadinejad's nuclear posture will be during his second presidential term, the possibility of confrontation instead of cooperation is so much more real. In facing this reality, creativity and maturity need to prevail to avoid an escalation that leads to a no-win endgame.

Iran's Regional Ambitions

Complicating matters further are Iran's calculations that a nuclear capability will help it fulfill its regional ambitions. Salehi, when saying that the "importance of Iran's status in the region is obvious,"[5] echoes the sentiments of a broad segment of Iranian society. He talks of Iran possessing "the golden key in the region." This key to which he alludes has physical and historical attributes. Iran's geostrategic position and its imperial legacy propel Iran to pursue regional hegemony.

Iran is the only country with access to the Caucuses, Middle East, Central and South Asia, the Caspian Sea, the Persian Gulf, and the open seas. From a hydrocarbon perspective, with its location and vast amounts of oil and natural gas, Iran has the potential of being one of the most, if not the most, influential supplier and transportation hub of oil and gas not only in the region, but also in the global market. However, as Sadjadpour points out, Iranian assets have been plagued

---

4. "Iran's Nuclear Dossier Must be Closed: AEOI Director," *Tehran Times*, 19 July 2009 (http:www.tehrantimes.com/NCms/2007.asp?code=199120).
5. Ibid.

by mismanagement, and this, coupled with the sanctions and political tensions, has resulted in Iran becoming "a perennial underperformer." Shercliff posits that Iran could assume its natural position as the key country in hydrocarbon production, transportation, and politics if it would accept the "refreshed" E3+3 package, which remains on the table since offered in June 2008.

Beyond geography, Iran's narrative of Persian expansionism and destined leadership in the region, led by Ayatollah Ruhollah Musavi Khomeini's message "of spreading the revolution and establishing the Islamic Republic's preeminence," continues to resonate with the Iranian population.[6] This imperial collective identity remains and has been reinvigorated with the removal of the Saddam Hussein and the Taliban. Milani argues that this shift in regional politics has expedited Iran's regional ambitions and that the current situations in Afghanistan and Iraq present an opportunity for cooperation between the United States and Iran, assuming that the two parties can overcome their inherent distrust and recognize that their strategic interests lie on the same path forward. It would appear that some of these fears have yet to be conquered, as Sadjadpour indicates that Iran continues to be identified as the principal source of instability in Iraq.

One voice absent from this discussion is that of Iran's Arab neighbors, due to a late cancellation of the Arab presenter at the symposium. The Arab states should not be expected to take sitting down Iran's regional ambitions and its interest and influence in Iraq. Iran's involvement in Iraq and Lebanon and with Palestinian groups such as Hamas, coupled with its nuclear pursuits, has created noise in many Arab capitals. Ahmadinejad's 2007 offer to help fill the security vacuum that would be created when Western forces leave Iraq remains on the table and has been met with skepticism and suspicion from Iran's neighbors.[7]

---

6. Ray Takeyh, *Hidden Iran: Paradox and Power in the Islamic Republic* (New York: Times Books, 2006), 11. Takeyh uses Arab states rather than all of Iran's neighboring states.

7. See Amin Tarzi, "The World's Ninth Nuclear Power: Iran's Ambitions in the Middle East and Beyond," *Turkish Policy Quarterly* 6 (Summer 2007): 63 (http://www.turkishpolicy.com/images/stories/2007-02-centraleurasia/TPQ2007-2-tarzi.pdf).

As Ansari notes, the apparent rise in Iranian regional influence, spanning from Lebanon to Afghanistan, has emboldened Iran, and Milani reminds readers of the power that perception wields in politics. As Iran plans its course, it needs to recognize how the region and the world perceive its regional ambitions and pursuit of nuclear technology. Iran's posturing toward Israel and its fiery politics take on a new dimension when coupled with the threat of a nuclear weapons capability. Iran needs to employ *maslehat* to determine its course of action and to ensure that the outcome affords Iran the prestige and status it desires and deserves. "We want Iran to calculate what I think is a fair assessment that if the U.S. extends a defense umbrella over the region, if we do even more to support the military capacity of those in the Gulf," Secretary of State Hillary Rodham Clinton said in Phuket, Thailand, in July 2009. "It's unlikely that Iran will be any stronger or safer, because they won't be able to intimidate and dominate, as they apparently believe they can, once they have a nuclear weapon."[8]

The authors' expertise and in-depth analysis broaden and deepen the available discourse on Iran and provide context and guidance for confronting the Iranian nuclear issue. As revealed through their work, the Iranian puzzle piece is complex and demands close examination to ascertain its rightful place within the global puzzle.

---

8. Mark Landler, "Clinton Hints at 'Defense Umbrella' to Deter Iran," *New York Times*, 23 July 2009 (http://www.nytimes.com/2009/07/23/world/asia/23diplo.html?).

Iranian Power Structure

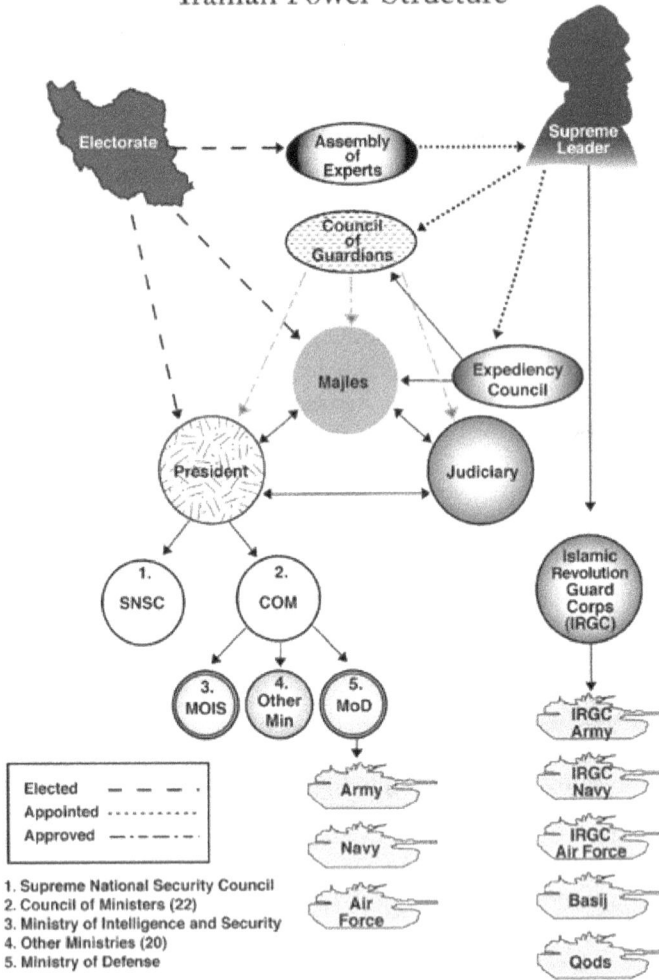

Legend:
- Elected — — — ·
- Appointed ··········
- Approved —·—·—·—

1. Supreme National Security Council
2. Council of Ministers (22)
3. Ministry of Intelligence and Security
4. Other Ministries (20)
5. Ministry of Defense

Guardian Council—Body of twelve jurists that approves candidates for the Assembly of Experts, parliament, and the presidency and determines whether laws passed by the *Majles* are in line with the constitution and Islamic law. Six members are selected by the supreme leader and the other six are appointed by the *Majles*.

Expediency Council—Council selected by the supreme leader that serves to facilitate and streamline resolutions over disagreements between the *Majles* and the Guardian Council, as well as to advise the supreme leader.

Assembly of Experts—Group of elected clerics tasked with selecting and reviewing the actions of the supreme leader.

Chapter 1
Iran Under Ahmadinejad

Ali M. Ansari

Mahmud Ahmadinejad was elected as the president of the Islamic Republic of Iran in 2005 promising to rid the government of the corruption that had accrued since the death of Ayatollah Ruhollah Musavi Khomeini in 1989, to pursue social and economic justice, and to return to the values of the early revolution. Armed with the self-confidence of a man immersed in religious convictions and an unshakable self belief, Ahmadinejad approached government with the reckless abandon of an iconoclast. It was an approach that proved as popular with the disenfranchised as much as it horrified the intellectual and bureaucratic elite, many of whom were likewise dismayed by the failures of the Islamic Republic and the unaccountability of the revolutionary organs in particular but felt that wholesale overhaul portended by the incoming president threatened to undermine the very foundations of a somewhat fragile political and economic system.

While it is true that Ahmadinejad found himself facing the natural inertia of any established system, he nonetheless spent the better part of the first term of his presidency reshaping the government of the Islamic Republic in his own image, in large measure supported by the office of Supreme Leader Ayatollah Sayyed Ali Hoseyni Khamenei, for whom Ahmadinejad's public obsequiousness and ideological world view have proven attractive. Perhaps more importantly, the dramatic rise in oil prices enabled Ahmadinejad to play the role of populist and to disguise the many fissures within the system under a torrent of oil money, which he injected into the economy with very little rhyme or reason.[1] Iranian economists protested that this

---

1. The price of crude oil rose from $35 per barrel in January 2005 to highs of around $140 during the summer of 2008, only to fall back to around $35 by the end of the year. Historical oil price data here and throughout the article is from U.S. Department of Energy, Energy Information Agency, "Petroleum Navigator" (http://tonto.eia.doe.gov/dnav/pet/hist/wtotworldw.htm).

lack of planning simply ensured a massive and unplanned injection of capital into an economy that could not sustain it, fueling inflation and a housing boom, which, in a scenario familiar to the West, has encouraged people to believe that real economic growth has in fact been taking place. They further warned that the drawing down of the oil reserve fund—built up by the administration of former president Sayyed Mohammad Khatami (1997-2005)—and the development of budgets dependent on ever higher receipts from oil would simply make the economy more vulnerable to a sudden reduction in the oil price. Ahmadinejad, buoyed by his own apparent popularity and an international environment that appeared to flaunt American failure in the region, dismissed these and other criticisms of his administration as the idle ranting of orthodox thinkers who had failed to appreciate his innate and instinctive genius.

Ahmadinejad is a product of the Khatami reform movement in more ways than one.[2] In an obvious sense, his emergence, and the ideals he represents, reflect a complete rejection of the reform process and the personality of Khatami in particular. Ahmadinejad himself takes the distinction further by distancing himself not only from Khatami but from the administration of former president Ali Akbar Hashemi Rafsanjani (1989-1997), to whom he ascribes much of the economic ills of the country. Yet as Ahmadinejad's presidency rejects much of the economic policy and planning of the previous sixteen years, his populism also reflects a profound desire to overturn the popularity of his immediate predecessor, a popularity that the hard right in Iran has resented and regarded as a perversion of the true values of the revolution. Defining these values and debating the legacy of the founder of the revolution, Ayatollah Khomeini, have been the stock and trade of the politics of the Islamic Revolution, and the claim that Rafsanjani and Khatami represented a loss of revolutionary focus is dubious to say the least.

---

2. Editor's Note: The reform movement (1997-2005) was the political momentum behind President Khatami's terms in office. The movement promised to bring greater freedom and democracy to Iranian politics and government, and the failure of its efforts has given strength to its conservative detractors. See Ray Takeyh, *Hidden Iran: Paradox and Power in the Islamic Republic* (New York: Times Books, 2006), 44-45.

One of the striking anomalies of the hard right Principle-ist challenge is that it does not have the support of many of Khomeini's closest supporters, allies, and family members.[3] Indeed, the Principle-ist challenge can be better interpreted as the attempt by Khamenei to supplant the founder of the revolution as the leading light of revolutionary ideology. It is quite clear that there is a tight and highly dependent relationship between Khamenei and the Principle-ist faction. This is not simply an ideological relationship, but a partnership in the consolidation of power, and it is important to recognize this relationship as one of mutual dependence. This interdependence explains the continued and critical support provided by the supreme leader for the president and his government, even when other conservatives have increasingly criticized the president's incoherent policies.

Another factor also helps explain this support, and it reflects the personality of the supreme leader as much as his political relationship with Ahmadinejad. Khamenei is haunted by the example of the last shah, Mohammad Reza Shah Pahlavi, who is generally considered to have lost his throne through indecisiveness and weakness. Consequently, Khamenei has sought to overcompensate for what is generally regarded to be his political and theological weakness by appearing and behaving in a manner that is both interventionist and resolute. In such a climate, considerable credence is given to not changing one's mind and to appearing consistent. The immediate consequence of this approach, of course, is that Khamenei is likely to continue supporting Ahmadinejad long after most observers consider it prudent or necessary. This support is mutual, and in rejecting his predecessors' policies, Ahmadinejad emphatically allied himself with the supreme leader, to whom he has shown an unprecedented public deference. If Rafsanjani and Khatami enjoyed difficult relationships

---

3. Editor's Note: The Principle-ists are the religious and social conservative factions that opposed the liberal policies of former President Khatami. They arose as the result of Khatami's reform efforts and are now a considerable political conservative force. See Ali M. Ansari, *Iran Under Ahmadinejad: The Politics of Confrontation.* Adelphi Paper 393. (Abingdon, U.K.: Routledge for the International Institute for Strategic Studies, 2007), 32; Raz Zimmt, "The 2008 Iranian Parliamentary Elections: A Triumph of the System," *Middle East Review of International Affairs* 12 (June 2008): 41-43.

with Khamenei, whom they regarded as little more than the first among equals, if that, Ahmadinejad—in public at least—has been very clear about the nature of the hierarchy.

Ahmadinejad's domestic agenda and the realignment of power were ably facilitated by highly fortuitous circumstances both with respect to the economy and the international environment. In 2005, Ahmadinejad inherited a nuclear crisis, which, after two years of tortuous negotiations, had not reached a satisfactory conclusion. The details of this process can be found elsewhere, but suffice it to say that both Iran and the parties with which it negotiated share the blame for the failure of progress by 2005.[4] It is with no little irony that it was only at this late date that the Europeans had convinced the United States to take a much more visible role in the negotiations, at the very time when the inauguration of Ahmadinejad represented a shift away from negotiations for the Iranians encouraged not only by the failures of the Khatami administration, but also by the realization that the U.S. position in the Middle East was no longer as robust or confident as it had been in 2003. Ahmadinejad argued that Iran could only achieve the results it wanted by being robust and confrontational, that the willingness to compromise was taken as a sign of weakness of the administration of U.S. President George W. Bush, and perhaps most importantly, that by 2005, America's room for maneuver was considerably more limited.

There were many within the Iranian political elite who accepted this general assessment, arguing that Khatami's good will had largely been rejected and that the United States only respected force. Ahmadinejad's approach was reinforced by a world view that took this analysis a stage further. While some viewed the change to a more confrontational stance as tactical rather than strategic—a means to securing an end— for Ahmadinejad, this shift represented deeper ideological convictions that drew on a Marxist understanding of global politics that pointed

---

4. For the nuclear issue, see Simon Shercliff's essay, which is chapter 4 of this book, as well as the International Atomic Energy Agency's site, "In Focus: IAEA and Iran" (http://www.iaea.org/NewsCenter/Focus/IaeaIran/index.shtml).

to the inevitable collapse of capitalism. For Ahmadinejad, the politics of confrontation was not a means to a redefined relationship, but a means to revolutionizing the international system in Iran's favor. Such a grandiose vision, which was derided and ridiculed by his political opponents, struck a chord with an overwhelmingly nationalistic population eager for international stature and success. Indeed, for all his religious heterodoxy, Ahmadinejad found nationalism and its accompanying rhetoric far more intoxicating for both the Iranian public and for himself.

With the apparent growth in Iranian power throughout the region, from Afghanistan to Lebanon—a consequence of Western incoherence more than real Iranian strength—Ahmadinejad's belief in himself seemed justified and became contagious. The more people believed, the more the critics were silenced, and the more Ahmadinejad's self belief was reinforced. Much is said about Ahmadinejad's incorruptibility, especially in contrast to some members of the political elite, yet while this may allude to financial probity (an aspect that has come under increasing scrutiny of late), it was very clear from quite early in his presidency that Ahmadinejad was easily overcome by the possibilities and perks of power. This bent was not only reflected in his highly personal choices for government posts, with officials chosen mainly for the personal loyalty to the man (Ahmadinejad) and mission rather than professional competence, but also in his obvious contempt for what remained of process and procedure. Ahmadinejad's disdain for the *Majles* (the Iranian parliament) was especially irksome to the hard-line deputies who had done so much to see him elected. Rather than face questions in parliament, Ahmadinejad was far happier playing the role of leader, either on the world stage in front of an international media, who seemingly thirsted after his every statement, or in lavish provincial tours in which he performed for adoring masses in increasing desperation for some sort of hope and salvation. Ahmadinejad clearly relished the role, and a dependency culture emerged between a people in need and a leader who craved attention.

Facilitating this process was the availability of enormous amounts of oil revenue. When Khatami came into office in 1997, oil stood at approximately $17 per barrel. It had dropped to the $10-12 range by the spring of 1998. Consequently, Khatami was forced to approach the economy with a degree of prudence and austerity. The lack of finance meant that he was unable to push through many of the ideas he had envisaged for the transformation of the Iranian economy. Ultimately, Khatami's economic legacy was managing a bad economy well, and as oil prices gradually rose, he left a growing oil reserve fund to be set aside for possible downturns in the economy and for investment in large infrastructural projects.

Ahmadinejad entered office with oil at around $60 a barrel and without much idea of economic planning or policy. Khatami had left a strategic plan for the next twenty years, although it was so vague as to allow any subsequent president considerable room for maneuver. Ahmadinejad and his allies, who were eager to consolidate power and to eradicate the popularity of Khatami among the people, used the funds to effectively buy the public. The days of austerity were over; oil money was provided to every citizen. The availability of such large amounts of money also allowed Ahmadinejad to indulge in theatrical politics on a scale not seen since the days of the last shah. Not only did he embark on a series of expensive provincial tours, he also used these "meet the people" expeditions to distribute cash, raise salaries, and announce dramatic initiatives, many of which had not been budgeted or were administratively difficult to achieve.

In the early days of his presidency, criticism of these adventures in the countryside was relatively muted, but it did not take long for contrary voices to be heard. Both conservatives and professionals raised concerns over Ahmadinejad's policies, including an extensive critique of his lack of economic planning issued by fifty-seven economists, who warned of the dire consequences of the massive injection of liquidity into the economy.[5] More damning than their economic critique, which warned

---

5. "Namah-ye chaharome eqtesad-danan be ra'is-e jomhur" [Fourth Letter of Economists to the President], *Mardom-Salari*, 22 December 2007 (http://www.mordomsalari.com/Template1/Article.aspx?AID=2397).

of high inflation and property speculation, was their observation that the president seemed uninterested in any professional advice, appeared to appoint officials on the basis of ideology, and moreover, boasted about his "instinctive" and "anti-intellectual" approach to government. Ahmadinejad not only dismissed such comments but also sought to present himself as a new type of revolutionary intellectual with access to radical ideas. One of his supporters argued that people did not understand the president because he moved at the speed of a "phantom jet," with the idea clearly being that Ahmadinejad operated on an altogether different plane of thought.

The antiestablishment posture worked for a time, but problems were bound to arise once the masses, whose loyalty he craved, began to suffer through the high inflation his policies were promoting. Ahmadinejad sought to ascribe these problems to international sanctions, but few commentators within the country believed this argument. When the *Majles* criticized the rise in prices of everyday goods, Ahmadinejad simply resorted to a swift dismissal of the criticisms as either politically unfounded or ignorant. His ability to remain on this path depended on two factors: the continued support of the supreme leader, who had effectively entered into a dependent relationship with him; and the continued rise in the price of oil. Indeed, even government officials and ostensible allies of the president grew weary and warned of the excessive dependence on rising oil prices. In April 2008, Interior Minister Mostafa Pour-Mohammadi, a noted hard-liner, resigned his post, citing differences that were later revealed to be concerns that the president had illegally raided the oil reserve fund.

News that the oil reserve fund has been severely depleted over the last few years has come as a considerable shock to Iranians. While precise figures remain vague, the inadvertent leak from a government minister that the fund stood at $9 billion in the fall of 2008 resulted in immediate attempts at damage limitation control from the government, which countered with an estimate of $25 billion.[6] This figure still is considerably lower than the $82 billion that the government was

---

6. "Iran: Oil under $60 Troubling for the Economy," *Fars New Agency,* 4 November 2008 (http://english.farsnews.net/newstext.php?nn=8708141516).

calculated to have had in March 2008, which would have provided a financial cushion in case of an oil price drop.[7] Indeed, although they publicly gloated at the collapse of Western financial institutions in September, it took little more than four weeks for Iranian officials to realize that the consequences of this global economic downturn would affect Iran in a concomitant deflation of the oil bubble. Within weeks, the price of oil dropped to below $60 a barrel, the price that had greeted Ahmadinejad on his inauguration, creating a situation for which the president had no answer.

Not surprisingly, recriminations followed. A particularly combative and boisterous *Majles* decided to impeach the minister of interior, Ali Kordan, for professing to hold an honorary doctorate from the University of Oxford. The impeachment is significant for a number of reasons. Ahmadinejad has to lose but one more minister (to dismissal or impeachment) to force a vote of confidence in his entire cabinet. Perhaps more importantly, it is no longer clear who will manage the forthcoming presidential elections (June 2009). Indeed, some are speculating that a combination of economic woes, a change of guard in the White House, and general disillusionment with Ahmadinejad among former allies, let alone the populace at large, will result in an opening up of the political contest.

Powerful voices in support of a renewed Khatami candidacy are already being heard.[8] However, much depends not only on developments in the economy, but on the attitude of the supreme leader, who finds himself in an increasingly awkward position. Most recently, he yet again came out in support of Ahmadinejad and his policies, thereby tying himself most emphatically to the cause. He can of course change his mind, if events force him to do so, but like all weak men, he places

---

7. Chip Cummins and Farnaz Fassihi, "Weaker Oil May Crimp Iran's Spending," *Wall Street Journal Online*, 25 October 2008 (http://online.wsj.com/article/SB122489443738668849.html).

8. Editor's Note: Khatami was the leading pro-reform candidate for the presidency until he withdrew from the race on 16 March 2009 citing the need for unity among reformists and pledging his support for former Prime Minister Mir-Hoseyn Musavi.

unusual emphasis on not changing his mind, confusing stubbornness with strength. In short, it will take a remarkable economic shock to shift him, and even then, it may be too late.

Chapter 2
Talking to Tehran: With Whom,
About What, and How?

Karim Sadjadpour

The long-standing policy debate about whether or not to "engage" Iran is now futile. In the post-September 11 world, Iran is integral to several issues of critical importance to the foreign policy of the United States, namely Iraq, Afghanistan, Arab-Israeli peace, terrorism, nuclear proliferation, and energy security. Shunning Iran will not ameliorate any of these issues, and confronting Iran militarily will exacerbate all of them. The only remaining option is talking to Tehran. The devil, however, is in the details. With whom in Iran should the U.S. talk? What should the U.S. talk to them about? And how should the U.S. talk to them?

For the last several years, U.S. policy toward Iran has focused almost exclusively on short-term tactics at the expense of a coherent strategy. The results are self-evident: today Iran is more repressive, its nuclear stance has grown more defiant, and its support for extremist groups has increased. This chapter will focus less on ways to punish troubling Iranian behavior and more on a strategy that attempts to modify Iranian policies, allay the long-standing enmity between Washington and Tehran, and facilitate internal political reform with Iran. It begins with four fundamental premises:[1]

> 1. Talking to Iran does not imply offering concessions, in no way implies appeasement of troubling Iranian behavior, and does not preclude efforts to simultaneously counter Iranian influence and policies that are problematic.

---

1. For a discussion of some of these premises, also see Ronald E. Neumann's essay, which is chapter 3 of this book.

2. The Islamic Republic is not on the verge of collapse, and any reform movement will require time to revive. Abrupt political change in Tehran is unlikely and would not necessarily be an improvement on the status quo, as the only groups that are both organized and armed in Iran are the Islamic Revolution Guard Corps (IRGC) and the Basij militia. More liberal political groups are unorganized and unarmed.

3. U.S. concerns about the Iranian behavior—whether it is nuclear ambitions, opposition to Israel, or support for extremist groups—will not be allayed as long as the status quo regime is in power in Tehran and its relations with Washington remain adversarial. In the current context, U.S. concerns that Iran is pursuing a clandestine nuclear weapons program will remain even if Iran were to announce suspension of uranium enrichment activities tomorrow.

4. The greatest impact Washington can have to help advance the causes of democracy, civil society, and human rights in Iran are policies that facilitate, rather than impede, Iran's path to modernization. Improved Iranian ties with the United States are a prerequisite to Iran's reintegration into the global economy, which would expedite internal political and economic reform in Iran and dilute rather than fortify hard-liners' control of power.

I. Who to Talk to

There is good reason why policy makers have often struggled to understand where and how power is wielded in Tehran. From the Islamic Republic's inception in 1979, the revolution's father, Ayatollah Ruhollah Musavi Khomeini, aimed to set up the government's power structure in a way that would make it impervious to foreign influence. This meant creating multiple power centers whose competition would provide checks and balances to prevent one branch or individual from becoming too powerful and susceptible to outside influence. The result has been frequent political paralysis, an inability to make big decisions, and a tendency to muddle along with entrenched policies.

The Power of Khamenei

While three decades later it remains difficult to discern why and how important decisions are made in Tehran, what can be said with confidence is that Supreme Leader Ayatollah Ali Hoseyni Khamenei is Iran's most powerful man. He may not make decisions unilaterally, but no major decisions can be taken without his consent. As supreme leader, he has constitutional authority over the main levers of state, namely the judiciary, military, and media. He also has effective control over the country's second most powerful institution, the Guardian Council, a twelve-member body (all of whom are directly or indirectly appointed by him) that has the authority to vet all electoral candidates and veto any parliamentary decisions.

Various domestic factors have made Khamenei's role in the consensus-building process greater than ever before: 1) a vast network of commissars stationed in strategic posts throughout government bureaucracies, dedicated to enforcing his authority; 2) the rapidly rising political and economic influence of the IRGC, whose top leaders are directly appointed by Khamenei; 3) the political disillusionment and disengagement of Iran's young population, prompted by the unfulfilled expectations of the reformist era;[2] 4) the 2005 election of hard-line President Mahmud Ahmadinejad, who trounced Khamenei's chief rival, former President Ali Akbar Hashemi Rafsanjani, in a second-round runoff; and 5) the conservative-dominated parliament, headed by Khamenei loyalist Ali Ardashir Larijani. Individuals who are either directly appointed by Khamenei or unfailingly obsequious to him currently lead the most influential institutions in Iran's byzantine power structure.

---

2. Editor's Note: The reform movement (1997-2005) was the political momentum behind President Khatami's terms in office. The movement promised to bring greater freedom and democracy to Iranian politics and government, and the failure of its efforts has given strength to its conservative detractors. See Ray Takeyh, *Hidden Iran: Paradox and Power in the Islamic Republic* (New York: Times Books, 2006), 44-45.

Externally, up to the fall of 2008, soaring oil prices together with Iran's expanded regional influence has given the Islamic Republic unprecedented power vis-à-vis the United States, offering Khamenei and Iran's hard-liners a newfound confidence. Iran's virtual encirclement by U.S. forces, efforts by the administration of U.S. President George W. Bush to promote democracy in Iran, and repeated threats of military action have combined to create a highly securitized atmosphere, allowing Tehran's hard-liners a further pretext to silence dissent and limit political and social freedoms.

While these factors are dynamic—oil prices may drop further, the state of Iraq may improve still, and Ahmadinejad may not be reelected president—for the foreseeable future, Iran will remain a vital influence on major U.S. interests, and Khamenei will continue to be the most critical figure in Iran.

What Does Khamenei Want?

Advocates of engagement often speak of the need for a bold U.S. gesture, a "Nixon to China" approach. Before this can happen, however, a fundamental question needs clarification: does Ayatollah Khamenei genuinely seek a modus vivendi with Washington? Or is enmity toward the United States necessary to retain the ideals of the revolution and the legitimacy of the Islamic Republic?

Khamenei's nineteen-year track record depicts a risk-averse leader— courting neither confrontation nor accommodation with the West— who is also saturated with mistrust.[3] He believes that Iran's strategic location and energy resources are too valuable to the United States to be controlled by an independent-minded Islamic government, hence Washington aspires to go back to the "patron-client" relationship existing at the time of the shah. In this context, whether U.S. officials announce they want to have a dialogue with Iran or to isolate it, Khamenei presumes nefarious intentions.

---

3. Editor's Note: Khamenei has been the supreme leader of Iran since 1989. Prior to this, he was the president of Iran from 1981 to 1989.

At the same time, the role of ideology and political expediency in Khamenei's anti-American worldview cannot be discounted. A conciliatory approach toward the United States and a nonbelligerent approach toward Israel would be parting ways with two of the three ideological symbols of the Islamic Republic (the other being the mandatory *hejab* for women). For Khamenei, if the Islamic revolution was all about momentous change, the years since have been about maintaining the revolutionary status quo. Nor is Khamenei's rationale purely ideological; his writings and speeches suggest that he agrees with Western advocates who argue that were Iran to open up to the United States, such engagement would spur major cultural, political, and economic reform.

For these reasons, as long as Khamenei remains supreme leader, a fundamental shift in Iranian domestic and foreign policy appears unlikely. Given that his selection as leader was based on his fealty to revolutionary ideals and the vision of Khomeini—whose political views crystallized in the anti-imperialist heyday of the 1960s and '70s—the chances of Khamenei being willing or able to reinvent himself at the age of seventy do not appear strong.

II. What to Talk About

> *There are few nations in the world with which the United States has less reason to quarrel or more compatible interests than Iran. . . . There is no American geopolitical motivation for hostility between Iran and the United States. . . . Iran is destined to play a vital—in some circumstances, decisive—role in the [Persian] Gulf and in the Islamic world. A prudent American government needs no instruction on the desirability of improving relations with Iran.*
>
> Henry A. Kissinger, *Does American Need a Foreign Policy?*[4]

---

4. Henry A. Kissinger, *Does America Need a Foreign Policy? Toward a Diplomacy for the 21st Century* (New York: Simon and Schuster, 2001), 196.

Iran scholars often debate to what degree the country's foreign policy is driven by national interests as opposed to revolutionary ideology. Examples of each abound. Invoking Islamic solidarity to support the Palestinian cause is consistent with Iran's revolutionary ideology, while ignoring Islamic solidarity in Chechnya for fear of antagonizing Russia is consistent with Iranian national interests.

Another interpretation of Iranian foreign policy is that it is a by-product of U.S.-Iran relations. According to this line of thinking, Iran is not inherently opposed to America, but it is driven by a sense of insecurity vis-à-vis the United States. Hence, when U.S.-Iran relations are most adversarial—as they have been the last several years—Tehran strives to make life difficult for the United States as a means of protecting itself. Iran's friendship with Venezuela's Hugo Chavez can be explained in this context.

The task of the U.S. President Barack H. Obama's administration should be to test whether a refined, conciliatory U.S. approach could compel Tehran to dilute, or perhaps even abandon, the revolutionary, anti-American aspect of its foreign policy in favor of a more cooperative working relationship with Washington. A survey of the issues of broad concern between the two countries—Iraq, Afghanistan, nuclear proliferation, terrorism, energy security, and Arab-Israeli peace—underscores former U.S. Secretary of State Henry Kissinger's argument that Washington and Tehran have much in common:

Iraq

While U.S. and Iranian interests in Iraq are certainly not identical, a good argument can be made that Washington has more overlapping interests with Tehran in Iraq than with any of Iraq's other neighbors:

Stability. Instability and carnage provide more fertile ground for radical Salafist groups—such as al-Qaeda—who are violently opposed to American, Iranian, and Shiite influence, and would also create an influx of Iraqi refugees to Iran.

Territorial Integrity. The implications of a partitioned Iraq—namely an independent Iraqi Kurdistan—are serious for Iran, which has its own disaffected Kurdish community. At the same time, both Washington and Tehran can live with a degree of Kurdish autonomy, which makes Turkey very uncomfortable.

Sectarian Harmony. Given its quest to be the vanguard of the largely Sunni-Arab Middle East, the last thing Iran wants to do is project Shiite power or stir Sunni resentment throughout the region.

Democracy. Given the Shiite demographic majority, Iran feels confident that elections are the best vehicle to assert its interests.[5] Fearing Shiite ascendancy in Baghdad, U.S. allies such as Saudi Arabia, Jordan, and Kuwait are far more concerned about a democratic Iraq.

Despite these overlapping interests, Iran's role in Iraq has been at best schizophrenic and at worst nefarious. Both U.S. military personnel and Iraqi officials have described Iran as a primary source of instability.

From Tehran's perspective, given that one of the underlying premises of the 2003 U.S.-led Iraq war was to change the political culture of the Middle East, it made little sense to Iran for it to play a cooperative or passive role in Iraq. On the contrary, believing that the United States was intent on installing in Baghdad a pro-American puppet regime sympathetic to Israel and hostile to Iran, Tehran had an incentive to try to make life difficult for the United States and ensure that its friends ascended to positions of power.

Afghanistan

Likewise in Afghanistan, Washington has more overlapping interests with Tehran than it does with allies Pakistan and Saudi Arabia:

Stability and economic reconstruction. Having accommodated more than 2 million Afghan refugees, Tehran does not stand to gain from

---

5. Editor's Note: According to the Central Intelligence Agency's "World Factbook," Shiites make up 60-65 percent of Iraq's population. They comprise 89 percent of Iran's population (https://www.cia.gov/library/publications/the-world-factbook/).

continued strife in Afghanistan and has sought to play a leading role in the country's reconstruction, ranking among the top ten aid donors.

Counter-narcotics. With one of the highest incidence of drug addiction in the world and a strict penal code prohibiting drug use, Iran has been highly vigilant in policing drug traffickers.[6]

Support for the government of Afghan President Hamid Karzai. While it has not abandoned its support for other allies in Afghanistan, Iran has been supportive of the Karzai government and made numerous pledges of security and economic cooperation.

Opposition to the Taliban. Iran nearly fought a war against the inherently anti-Shiite Taliban in 1998 and supported the opposition Northern Alliance long before September 11.

Similar to Iraq, however, in an effort to make life difficult for the United States, Tehran's behavior has been at times schizophrenic and counter to its own national interests. Iranian state radio programs broadcast in Afghanistan have referred to Karzai as the "stooge of the U.S.," but most egregious are accusations that Iran has provided support to its old nemesis the Taliban.[7]

Nuclear Proliferation

The impetus for Iran's nuclear ambitions remains nebulous. Is the country's clerical leadership fixed on acquiring a nuclear weapons capability in order to dominate the Middle East and threaten Israel? Is Iran a misunderstood and vulnerable nation driven by a need to protect itself from unstable neighbors and a hostile U.S. government? Or is Iran simply moving forward with its nuclear program to gain leverage with the United States?[8]

---

6. Editor's Note: According to the Central Intelligence Agency's "World Factbook," "Iran remains one of the primary transshipment routes for Southwest Asian heroin to Europe; suffers one of the highest opiate addiction rates in the world, and has an increasing problem with synthetic drugs" (https://www.cia.gov/library/publications/the-world-factbook/fields/2086.html?countryName=Iran&countryCode=IR&regionCode=me&#IR).

7. For example, see Amin Tarzi, "The World's Ninth Nuclear Power: Iran's Ambitions in the Middle East and Beyond," *Turkish Policy Quarterly* 6 (Summer 2007): 61-65.

8. For more on the nuclear issue see, Simon Shercliff's essay, which is chapter 4 of this book.

While threat perception, geopolitics, and national pride are important facets of Iran's nuclear ambitions, the nuclear issue is more a symptom of the deep mistrust between Washington and Tehran than the underlying cause of tension. The United States has no confidence that Iran's intentions are peaceful and believes that in light of Tehran's past nuclear indiscretions, hostility toward Israel, and support for extremist groups, it should not be permitted to enrich uranium (the process required for both a civilian nuclear energy program and a weapons program). Iran is equally convinced that Washington is opposed to its technological advancement and is using the nuclear issue as a pretext to confront it.

Ultimately, the nuclear issue will never be fully resolved absent a broader diplomatic accommodation between the two sides, wherein the United States alters its approach to Iran and Tehran alters its approach toward Israel. If there is one common goal that both the United States and Iran share, it is the avoidance of nuclear arms race in the Middle East.

Arab-Israeli Conflict

The greatest impediment to an improvement in U.S.-Iran relations is Tehran's position toward Israel. Whereas regarding the prospect of normalized relations with the United States, Iranian leaders have sometimes allowed room for ambiguity, Tehran's public rejection of the Jewish state has always been vociferous and unequivocal.

Iran's policy is a two-pronged approach of armed resistance as a prelude to a "popular referendum." Reasoning that "the Zionists have not pulled out of even a single square meter of occupied territories as a result of negotiation,"[9] Tehran openly supports militant groups such as Hamas and Islamic Jihad. But rather than seek Israel's physical destruction, Iran's proposed solution is a scenario whereby all inhabitants of Israel and the occupied territories—Jewish, Muslim, and Christian—would be given a vote to determine the country's future outlook. Given that Palestinians—including those in refugee camps—now constitute a

---

9. Karim Sadjadpour, *Reading Khamenei: The World View of Iran's Most Powerful Leader* (Washington D.C.: Carnegie Endowment for International Peace, 2008), 20.

demographic majority, Iran believes that a popular referendum would lead to the Jewish state's political dissolution.[10]

Yet behind Tehran's seemingly intractable position, an important caveat exists: Iran's leaders have long made it clear that they will accept any territorial solution agreed upon by the Palestinians.

Energy Security

With the world's second-largest oil and natural gas reserves, Iran's importance to the global energy market is self-evident.[11] Yet a variety of factors—mismanagement, sanctions, and political tension—have made Iran a perennial underperformer. Its oil output, around 4.2 million barrels per day, is far below the 6 million barrels it produced prior to the revolution, and while it has 15 percent of the world's natural gas reserves, it has only 2 percent of total production.[12]

Notwithstanding the political implications, the benefits of a U.S. energy relationship with Iran would be numerous. For one, energy cooperation between the two countries would decrease the political risk premium currently in established oil prices; increased Iranian supply to the market would likely reduce cost; and development of Iranian national gas reserves and pipelines would weaken the tremendous leverage Russia currently holds over Europe.

There are economic imperatives for Iran to cooperate with the United States as well. Given the combination of heavily subsidized

---

10. Editor's Note: This takes into account UN Resolution 242, which some argue grants Palestinian refugees the "Right of Return." This resolution is not recognized by Israel, and as Ruth Lapidoth has written, "Neither under the international conventions, nor under the major UN resolutions, nor under the relevant agreements between the parties, do the Palestinian refugees have a right to return to Israel." Ruth Lapidoth, "Do Palestinian Refugees Have a Right to Return to Israel?" Israeli Ministry of Foreign Affairs Web site, 15 January 2001 (http://www.mfa.gov.il/MFA/Peace+Process/Guide+to+the+Peace+Process/Do+Palestinian +Refugees+Have+a+Right+to+Return+to.htm).

11. Editor's Note: According to the U.S. Department of Energy's Energy Information Administration, Iran holds the world's third-largest proven oil reserves and the world's second-largest natural gas reserves. Energy Information Administration, "Iran Energy Profile" (http://tonto.eia.doe.gov/country/country_energy_data.cfm?fips=IR).

12. Ibid.

gasoline, rising domestic consumption, and stagnating or decreasing production due to infrastructure deterioration, Iran's oil exports are projected to drop.[13] If the trends continue—increased consumption and decreased output—Iran could conceivably be on the path to being a net oil importer.

Such a situation would force very painful decisions. Either the regime would have to cut gasoline subsidies—a difficult task for a president who ran on a populist platform—or the leadership would have to alter its policies to attract rather than repel outside investment. Most likely it will require a combination of both.

Terrorism

For more than a decade, Iran has been atop the State Department's list of "state sponsors of terror," due mainly to its support for Hezbollah and the Palestinian militant groups Hamas and Islamic Jihad. Absent either a Palestinian-Israeli settlement or a U.S.-Iranian diplomatic accommodation, this situation will likely continue. At the same time, however, Iran and the United States share a common enemy in the inherently anti-Shiite al-Qaeda.

III. How to Talk to Iran

The long-standing taboo about talking to America has seemingly been broken in Tehran. While just five years ago, individuals could be imprisoned in Iran for advocating dialogue with the United States, today Iran's president has written open letters to former President Bush and challenged him to debates.

Nonetheless, there are a variety of reasons why even a sincere, sustained American attempt to dialogue with Tehran may not bear fruit:

---

13. Editor's Note: According to the Central Intelligence Agency's "World Factbook," Iran produces 4.7 million barrels of oil per day and consumes 1.6. The country also produces 111.9 billion cubic meters of natural gas and consumes 111.8 billion cubic meters (https://www.cia.gov/library/publications/the-world-factbook/geos/IR.html).

• Historically, the Islamic Republic has tended to make difficult decisions only under duress. Intoxicated by their new-found standing, Iran's hard-liners may not feel compelled to make any compromises.

• Paralyzed by the competing ambitions of various factions and institutions, the Islamic Republic may prove incapable of reaching an internal consensus, falling back on long-entrenched policies.

• Unconvinced of U.S. intentions, the regime may shun increased ties with Washington, believing it to be a Trojan horse for a counterrevolution.

• Fearful of the unpredictable domestic change that an opening with the United States might catalyze, Iran's leadership may well perceive reconciliation with Washington as an existential threat.

To ensure the greatest possible chance of success, there are eight useful prescriptions the Obama administration should keep in mind when dealing with Iran:

1. Build Confidence on Areas of Common Interest

In the past, the one issue on which there is intense disagreement and seemingly no common ground—the Israeli-Palestinian conflict—has dominated the context of the U.S.-Iranian relationship and set the underlying tenor of distrust and ill will between the two sides.

Given that the fundamental source of tension between Washington and Tehran is mutual mistrust, confidence will be easier to build on areas of common interest, such as Iraq and Afghanistan, as opposed to areas of little or no common interest, such as the Palestinian-Israeli conflict or the nuclear issue. The Obama administration should seek to resume the U.S.-Iran discussions that the Bush administration initiated in Baghdad, while opening a similar channel of discussion in Kabul. Ideally, these talks can be gradually, quietly expanded to encompass the broader areas of contention.

2. Begin Cautiously

Timing is important. It is inadvisable for President Obama to immediately adopt a comprehensive engagement approach that could enhance Ahmadinejad's chances of reelection in Iran's June 2009 presidential elections.[14]

If there is one thing that Ahmadinejad's presidency has proven, it is that the institution of president in Iran has real power, influence, and responsibilities. Since his tenure began in August 2005, he has used that influence to amplify objectionable Iranian foreign practices, while domestically, he has curtailed political and social freedoms and shown a flagrant disregard for human rights. While Ahmadinejad's reelection would not entirely preclude the prospect of a U.S.-Iran diplomatic breakthrough, his mere presence could present an insurmountable obstacle to confidence-building with Tehran.

To be clear, even without a major U.S. overture, there is a decent likelihood that Ahmadinejad could be reelected. For one, a combination of political inertia and name recognition has helped incumbents win Iran's last three presidential elections. More importantly, elections in Iran are not free and open, and this particular election will be strongly influenced by the wishes of the supreme leader—who has been generally supportive of Ahmadinejad.

Nonetheless, just as his election in 2005 shocked the most seasoned observers, Ahmadinejad's defeat in 2009 is certainly a possibility. Given his considerable mismanagement of the economy, it will be difficult for Ahmadinejad to run on the platform of economic justice and populism

---

14. Editor's Note: In March 2009, U.S. President Barack H. Obama made an address to the people and leaders of Iran, who were celebrating Nowruz. Nowruz is the commemoration of the spring equinox in the northern hemisphere and is celebrated as the beginning of the new year in the Iranian world. In the address, Obama made a request that the two nations (Iran and the U.S.) begin a practice of constructive engagement. (Online at http://www.whitehouse.gov/the_press_office/Videotaped-Remarks-by-The-President-in-Celebration-of-Nowruz/).

that got him elected in 2005. A major overture from the United States before the elections take place could redeem Ahmadinejad's management style and increase his popularity, both in the eyes of the public and political elites, particularly Khamenei. For this reason, it is better to begin with cautious, limited engagement until Iran's domestic situation is clearer.

3. Deal with Those Who Hold Power

Successful engagement will require a direct channel of communication with the supreme leader's office, such as former Foreign Minister Ali Akbar Velayati, one of Khamenei's chief foreign policy advisors, or perhaps ultimately with the leader himself.

Khamenei must be convinced that the United States is prepared to recognize and respect the legitimacy of the Islamic Republic and must be disabused of his conviction that U.S. policy is to bring about regime change, not negotiate behavior change. What is more, Khamenei will never agree to any arrangement in which Iran is expected to publicly retreat or admit defeat, nor can he be forced to compromise through pressure alone. Besides the issue of saving face, he believes deeply that compromising in the face of pressure is counterproductive, as it projects weakness and only encourages greater pressure.

4. Speak Softly and Carry a Big Stick

The Obama administration should heed the wisdom of former U.S. President Theodore Roosevelt. While in the context of domestic U.S. politics, threatening violence against Iran has become a way of appearing tough on national security for Democrats and Republicans alike. In the last five years, such rhetoric has empowered Tehran's hard-liners and aggrandized Iran's stature on the streets of Cairo, Amman, and even Jakarta as the Muslim world's only brave, anti-imperialist nation that speaks truth to power. What is more, when oil prices jump with each threat against Iran, Iran's nuclear program and its financial patronage of Hezbollah and Hamas become less costly.

With its weekly "death to America" diatribes, the Iranian government is certainly complicit in engaging in bellicose rhetoric. The United States need not take its behavioral cues from an insecure, repressive, undemocratic regime. Instead of reciprocating a culture of threats and name-calling, the Obama administration should project the dignity and poise of a superpower rather than allow the Iranian regime to define the tenor of the public discourse. A rhetorically hostile U.S. approach allows Iran's leadership to paint the United States as an aggressor, both internationally and domestically, and absolve itself from responsibility for its largely self-inflicted isolation and soiled international reputation.

5. Do Not Let the Spoilers Set the Tenor

Though small in number, powerful cliques, both within Iran and among Iran's Arab allies, have entrenched economic and political interests in preventing U.S.-Iran reconciliation. Domestically, these actors recognize that improved Iranian ties with Washington would likely induce political and economic reforms and competition that would undermine the quasi-monopolies they enjoy in isolation.

Among Iran's Arab allies such as Hezbollah and Hamas, the prospect of a U.S-Iranian accommodation could mean an end to their primary source of funding. For this reason, when and if a serious dialogue commences, the spoilers will likely attempt to torpedo confidence-building efforts.

Their tactics vary. They may issue belligerent rhetoric, target U.S. soldiers and interests in Iraq or Afghanistan, or see to it that a shipment of arms originating from Iran on its way to south Lebanon or Gaza is "discovered." Their intention is to leave fingerprints in order to sabotage any chance of a diplomatic breakthrough.

If Washington ceases dialogue or confidence-building with Tehran in retaliation for an egregious act committed by the spoilers, they will have achieved their goal.

6. Be Discreet

When it comes to U.S.-Iranian interaction, empirical evidence has shown that covert discussions outside of public earshot have a greater success rate. Building confidence in the public realm will be difficult, as politicians from both sides will likely feel the need to issue harsh rhetoric in order to maintain appearances. In addition, the likelihood that spoilers can torpedo the process either through malicious rhetoric or action is more limited if they do not know about it.[15]

Recognizing that their regional influence derives in large part due to their defiance of the United States, Iran would likely prefer not to publicly advertise its discussions with the Americans.

7. Keep International Coalition Intact

More than any other actor, the United States has the capability to influence Iranian behavior, both for better and for worse. To the extent possible, however, it is essential that Washington attempt to maintain a common international approach toward Iran, especially regarding the nuclear issue. Tehran is highly adept at identifying and exploiting rifts in the international community, and diplomatic efforts to check Iran's nuclear ambitions will unravel if key countries approach Iran with competing red lines.

A common European Union-U.S. approach is imperative. Given their divergent national interests, it may not be possible to unite China and Russia behind the U.S. position, although Moscow certainly has an interest in avoiding the prospect of a nuclear-armed Iran within missile range. A more robust U.S. effort at direct dialogue with Tehran would assuage international concerns about U.S. intentions and send the signal to the EU, Moscow, and Beijing that the United States is serious about reaching a diplomatic resolution to this dispute, which will likely strengthen the health of the coalition.

---

15. For a different opinion on secrecy during negotiations, see Ronald Neumann's essay, which is chapter 3 of this book.

8. Have Realistic Expectations

Around the same time President Obama was inaugurated in January 2009, the Iranian revolution marked its thirty-year anniversary. Throughout these last three decades, the U.S.-Iran relationship has been mired in deep-seated mistrust and ill will on a myriad of issues. Mindful of this mutual skepticism, results will not be instantaneous. Such antagonism will not melt away after one, two, or even six meetings. The initial pace will likely be painfully slow as each side ascertains whether the other truly has good intentions.

Chapter 3
When U.S.-Iranian Negotiations Start:
A Primer

Ronald E. Neumann

Whether the United States should talk to Iran is fiercely debated. Rarely discussed are the obstacles a U.S. administration will face, and issues it must be prepared for, when the time does come to talk. Yet success or failure may well turn on just such matters.

Talking with enemies is a long tradition in diplomacy. This is so because unless defeat of the enemy is likely, some compromise is eventually needed. If total victory seems unlikely, discourse is useful. However, negotiations are not an end in themselves and may reveal that resolution is not possible. Nor are negotiations an alternative to conflict; both can be pursued simultaneously. Indeed, that was exactly how the United States negotiated independence from Great Britain. But that analogy should remind us that one may have conflict and discussions continuing side by side for long periods.

Advocates of talks tend to point to opportunities missed. Recent books have noted particularly an Iranian offer in May 2003 to enter into comprehensive talks.[1] Writers have pointed to the interests in common and suggested the possibility of a "grand bargain."[2] That is one possible outcome. But to attempt to reach a bargain without adequate advance reflection on how to overcome the problems that must be dealt with along the way is unlikely to lead to successful negotiations. And failure may be politically painful.

---

1. See Tarita Parsi, *Treacherous Alliance: The Secret Dealings of Israel, Iran, and the United States* (New Haven, Conn.: Yale University Press, 2007); and Barbara Slavin, *Bitter Friends, Bosom Enemies: Iran, the U.S., and the Twisted Path to Confrontation* (New York: St. Martin's Press, 2007).

2. The question of dealing with Iran on issues of common interest is addressed by Karim Sadjadpour in chapter 2 of this book.

True, there are some common interests, including the potential for stability in Iraq and Afghanistan. And each side has things to offer the other, including an end to support for terrorism and development of Iran's oil and gas resources without the impediment of U.S. hostility. However, it is important to remember is that each side wants things that the other will be most loath to concede. To reach an agreement, the United States will have to cut through massive amounts of suspicion, misunderstanding, legal obstacles, and the domestic political opposition each side will face.

Suspicions

That the United States does not trust Iran needs little proof. It is worth understanding that they may be equally mistrustful. The Iranian government believed the George H.W. Bush administration would open talks after the hostages in Lebanon were released, but that did not happen. The Six-plus-Two talks led to Iranian cooperation in negotiating the Afghan peace arrangements of the Bonn Accord but withered thereafter.[3] The Iranian offer of 2003 appears to have met without even the courtesy of a response. For Iran, the present demand for nuclear preconditions to talk may look very much like a continuation of a familiar pattern in which U.S. willingness to engage disappears once U.S. goals are achieved. This does not mean that a deal cannot be reached, but it does suggest that preconditions will be hard to achieve and that Iran will seek guarantees from the United States, and vice versa.

Domestic suspicions and political opposition will complicate matters for each side. There remain Iranian elements with a deeply entrenched ideological opposition to talking with the United States. Talks themselves, and any arrangement reached, will potentially be a political stick that various Iranian opposition elements will find convenient to attack whoever is conducting the talks. Whatever the complexion of

---

3. These talks involved Afghanistan's six neighboring countries plus the United States and Russia.

the Iranian government that enters into talks, it will be aware of this. Thus the domestic pressures on the Iranian side to reach a deal that can be justified as heavily in favor of Iran will be large.

The same will be true in reverse for a U.S. administration. Particularly after the disputed Iranian presidential election, there will be many in the U.S. domestic political arena ready to criticize the fact of talks, and even more any outcome that seems to "reward terrorism" or to surrender U.S. positions, especially on the nuclear issue. Finding an agreement that each side can defend successfully to its own domestic critics is going to be intensely difficult. The concessions needed by one side will be exactly the "giveaways" for which the other will be attacked. In the Americans' case, this issue will be intensified by the probability that some issues to be settled may need legislation either to provide new arrangements or to remove old sanctions.

The "Larger" Issues

What one might call the major issues are much discussed in this book. In this chapter, it suffices to note them briefly. The biggest is of course the nuclear issue.[4] Close behind it comes Iranian support for terrorism, particularly for Hezbollah and Hamas.[5] For the Iranians, these groups are major geostrategic allies. While changes in Iraq and Afghanistan have removed major threats to Iran, it has no trusted friends on its borders. Iran is distrusted by the Sunni Arab regimes of the region and worries that U.S. troops could use its forces on Iran's borders for a future attack. What level of U.S. concessions would Iran ask for from the United States for Iran to surrender or weaken ties to its allies? It is not known.

Then there is Iranian support for insurgents in Iraq and Afghanistan. For Iran, these issues look different. Fighting two wars ties up the United States and reduces the odds that it will use force against Iran.

---

4. See Simon Shercliff's essay, which is chapter 4 in this book.
5. Editor's Note: For more on Iran's support of Hezbollah and Hamas and its perception within Israel, see Gerald M. Steinberg's essay, which is chapter 6 in this book.

What manner of guarantees will Iran seek to reduce what it may see as a potential threat from the United States? It is doubtful that Iran would simply trust promises from the U.S. as sufficient and equally doubtful that the U.S. would willingly give Iran a voice in limiting American troop numbers or deployments in either country.

None of this is meant to suggest that answers cannot be found over time. It is simply a reminder that finding solutions to the major issues in a bargain will be difficult, and that the odds of failure or impasse are at least as good as those of success.

The "Lesser" Issues

There are a host of issues on which Iran has been insisting for many years. Each could be a deal breaker for a U.S. administration. One is the Iranian demand for the payment of the so-called "frozen accounts" held by the United States since the hostage affair in Tehran (4 November 1979 to 29 January 1981). In reality, there are no bank accounts as such. All of the blocked accounts were released at the time of the Algiers declaration that settled the hostage crisis.[6] There may be some limited funds held by the U.S. Treasury. However, most of what is at issue are Iranian claims for payments made for U.S. military equipment either never built or never delivered. In many cases, the money went to U.S. contractors in settlement of claims. The claims now amount to between $20 and $30 billion, depending on interest calculations. There are some 1,100 such cases. In the 30 years since the Iran-United States Claims Tribunal at The Hague went to work to resolve disputed claims (as part of the Algiers Accords that freed the hostages), only 130 of these cases have been submitted to the tribunal, and none of them have been heard or resolved.[7] Expecting the tribunal process to resolve these 1,100 cases in anything like the time needed for a political settlement is unrealistic. So too is an expectation that the Iranians are likely to accept waiting many more years for one of their

---

6. Editor's Note: For a review of U.S.-Iranian relations, including the hostage crisis, see Kenneth Katzman, *U.S.-Iranian Relations: An Analytic Compendium of U.S. Policies, Laws and Regulations* (Washington, D.C.: Atlantic Council of the United States, 1999).

7. For an overview and a database of the claims, see the site for the Iran-United States Claims Tribunal (http://www.iusct.org/).

largest (and politically most sensitive) issues to be resolved. Assuming at least some of the Iranian claims are sustained, the U.S. paying them may require the use of appropriated funds. Congress may not agree.

Additionally, the Iranians have brought new claims for damages inflicted by U.S. sanctions that they claim are in violation of the Algiers Accords. They have also alleged that U.S. covert actions have caused damages and that these too are in violation of the accords. It is not known whether these are serious claims or bargaining positions.

Another particularly troubling issue will be the private claims of U.S. citizens upheld by U.S. courts against Iran on grounds of terrorism. Some estimates of these claims put them in the neighborhood of $16 billion in compensatory damages and perhaps another $25 billion in punitive damages. An additional $50 billion or so in such judgments relate to Iranian actions in Iraq.[8]

Iran has never recognized U.S. jurisdiction. It is unlikely to do so now and still less likely to pay such claims. Unless the issue is settled, a wide variety of U.S. and international businesses and even some international organizations could find their assets under threat in the United States for settlement of these damages. It is highly unlikely that Iran would close a deal on other matters and leave itself vulnerable to pressure from this source.

There would be no shortage of congressional voices ready to defend American citizens and U.S. court judgments from "giveaways to terrorists." An American administration that begins negotiations would be well-advised to have thought through this issue and found some negotiating ideas.

Other troublesome issues may arise. The Iranians previously wanted the United States to turn over leaders from the *Mujahdin-e-Khalq*

---

8. I am indebted to the Legal Advisor's office at the U.S. Department of State for background on these legal issues. Figures are estimates, but the order of magnitude makes the point.

(MEK) that are held in loose confinement in Camp Ashraf in Iraq.[9] Forced turnover would probably be illegal under international law be, opposed by human rights groups, and meet with at least some congressional opposition. MEK leaders have officially passed into Iraqi custody, but the Iranians may believe that the United States will be unable to control the Iraqis and, thus, this issue may not yet be removed from the debate. But that is not yet certain, and so far it remains an Iranian counter to U.S. requests for the surrender of al-Qaeda members held by Iran.

The Legal Structure

Some U.S. sanctions on Iran have been codified in law, while others are contained in a series of executive orders.[10] While in theory the executive branch has considerable freedom to change these sanctions, there will be a variety of forces intent on maintaining them, and they may lobby intensely for congressional action to put more of the sanctions into laws. Interested parties will range from committed proponents of overthrowing the Iranian regime to California pistachio growers wanting to protect their market.[11]

A U.S. administration that reaches a deal with Iran will have to persuade Congress to remove sanctions or not extend them over executive branch statements that their intent has been met. This in turn will increase pressures on the administration to show it has gained

---

9. Editor's Note: According to Acting Deputy Department Spokesman Gordon Duguid of the U.S. State Department, "the disposition of Camp Ashraf was given a full transfer to the responsibility of the Iraqis on February the 20th [2009]." He went on to say, "responsibility for resolving the situation at the camp rests with the Government of Iraq at this time." For the full statement, see the Daily Press Briefing, 30 March 2009 (http://www.state.gov/r/pa/prs/dpb/2009/03/120983.htm).

10. Relevant laws and executive orders are summarized by the U.S. Department of the Treasury, Office of Foreign Assets Control, in a January 2009 document, "Iran: What You Need to Know about U.S. Economic Sanctions" (http://www.ustreas.gov/offices/enforcement/ofac/programs/iran/iran.pdf).

11. When sanctions on Iranian pistachios were lifted during the Clinton administration's effort to reach out to Iran, California growers managed in effect to maintain them through intensive lobbying that retained prohibitive duties dating from 1985 based on an allegation of dumping. See John Lancaster, "Pistachio Diplomacy," *Washington Post*, 23 March 2000; and Scott Peterson, "Iran's Prized, and Political, Nuts," *Christian Science Monitor*, 2 December 1999. I am also indebted to professors W. Scott Harrop and Rouhollah K. Ramazani for further updates.

a victory in the negotiations. Grand bargains and one-sided victories are uneasy bedfellows.

Negotiating Styles and Starting Points

With so many domestic political perils awaiting, there may be a desire for secret talks. This was a repeated idea when Iran flirted with contacts during the Clinton administration.[12] It may be again.[13] However, it is a temptation that should be avoided since the probability of leaks from one side or the other is high, and the results are usually to put one or both governments on the defensive with domestic critics. The United States may, and probably should, try to keep the content of negotiations under wraps but should avoid the vulnerability of trying to keep the talks themselves secret.

The secrecy issue is but one example of the difference in styles and starting points between Washington and Tehran. While a new U.S. administration may have different tactics, the U.S. tendency in negotiations has usually been to precede them with extensive interdepartmental negotiations (the interagency process). Departments of State, Defense, Homeland Security, and Justice are likely to have different views in regard to negotiations with Iran. This is akin to negotiating with oneself before negotiating with others.

The result is that U.S. negotiators often lack flexibility, and negotiations can stall for long periods while the U.S. government fights within itself. Some administrations have tried to avoid this by negotiating in great secrecy from most of the government. Sometimes this works. U.S. Secretaries of State James A. Baker III and Henry A. Kissinger were masterful in this regard. But poorly handled, the results of such an approach produced the Iran-Contra scandal, complete with a key-

---

12. I was Iran Country Director for part of this time. Our answer that we could only pledge best efforts at confidentiality but not promise it was for us an honest answer, recognizing the probability of leaks. The Iranians seemed to regard the response as a trap, leaving us free to leak on purpose to weaken them at a time of our choosing.

13. Editor's Note: See also Karim Sadjadpour's essay, chapter 2 of this book.

shaped cake and a Bible.[14] Only strong presidential leadership can steer through such problems.

American negotiators tend to start from interests. The inclination is to list what is wanted and what can be given and then to try it out on representatives of the other side. From their reactions, negotiators then try to judge how to repackage the deal and what shifts they may have to accommodate. Having watched Iranians negotiate off and on for three decades, my guess is that the Iranian style will be very different. They will hold out vaguely worded promises in return for specific concessions, and later, the promises may dissolve when one tries to grasp them. Deals may seem close, only to fall apart as new demands or issues are advanced.

Americans may see such tactics as bad faith. For the Iranians, it is a matter of testing to see how firm or weak the other side is, whether it can be manipulated, and whether it is in so much of a hurry to reach agreement that it will make foolish concessions.

Iranians place great emphasis on "respect." Persian culture has complicated and deeply ingrained habits of speech and manners to show respect for person and position in social interaction that are very foreign to American habits of frankness and direct speech. Ignorant negotiators can easily find themselves at cross purposes, particularly since the overheated public rhetoric in each country's domestic discourse is unlikely to be controllable. The Iranian government is likely to react harshly—in American eyes perhaps disproportionately—to phrases like "Axis of Evil." Misunderstandings arising from these stylistic differences can arouse anger and confusion.

This Iranian style is all the more likely if they misunderstand a U.S. decision to negotiate after years of refusal. Iranian analysis is likely

---

14. Editor's Note: "These operations [Iran-Contra] were the provision of assistance to the military activities of the Nicaraguan contra rebels during an October 1984 to October 1986 prohibition on such aid, and the sale of U.S. arms to Iran in contravention of stated U.S. policy and in possible violation of arms-export controls." See Lawrence E. Walsh, "Final Report of the Independent Counsel for Iran/Contra Matters," U.S. Court of Appeals for the District of Columbia Circuit, 4 August 1993 (online at http://www.fas.org/irp/offdocs/walsh/).

to be along the lines that when the United States felt strong, it made demands. Now that it is in trouble in Iraq, Afghanistan, Lebanon, and in seeking an Arab-Israeli peace, it is weak and willing to pay heavily for Iranian support. Simply working through such preconceptions may be very time consuming and frustrating for the unprepared.

What to Do

The preceding catalogue of difficulties suggests neither that negotiations should not take place, nor that they cannot succeed. It does suggest certain conclusions.

First, negotiations must have strong presidential support and guidance. Without this, they will flounder in a morass of interagency differences, leaks, and domestic pressures.

Second, talks should be preceded by careful consideration within the administration of how far the United States might go in meeting Iranian demands. It is probably unwise to try for full interagency agreement, as it is likely to come at the cost of inflexible negotiating positions. But a president should have some idea of the problems negotiations will encounter and the price he might have to pay.

Third, the American public and the Congress need to be told frankly not only why the United States and Iran are talking, but that we expect talks to be long, possibly lasting years, that they will be difficult, and that essential interests will not be forfeited.

Fourth, neither talks nor pressures should be hostage to the other. To paraphrase former Israeli Prime Minister Yitzhak Rabin, the United States needs to negotiate as if there were no conflict and struggle as if there were no talks. The alternatives are either failed talks or a position of great weakness if every confrontation is hobbled by fears that it will undermine talks. The Iranians have mastered this quite traditional method of diplomacy, and the United States and its allies must do likewise.

Fifth, it is advisable to start slowly, exploring with the Iranians where there may be areas suitable for agreement. There have not been bilateral negotiations about a broad range of issues for years. Guesswork constitutes much of what Americans assume in the Iranian position, and the same is true of the Iranian assumptions. Haste will only convey weakness and misestimating of what is possible. Proceedings should be neither timid nor harsh, but should proceed slowly, identifying issues and problems, and trying to understand the Iranians and repay them in kind. Only from such a process can negotiators judge whether to pursue a great bargain or a series of smaller steps and agreements.

Finally, managing complicated allied relationships will not be an easy task. America's European allies, and even the Russians and Chinese, have been partners in joint positions toward Iran. The Gulf Arabs fear Iranian claims to hegemony in the Persian Gulf. Israel has strong views about the danger Iran poses for Israeli security. If U.S. consultation is deemed too little, suspicion will be intense and have ramifications in many other areas. If consultation is too broad, negotiations may become hostage to too many conflicting views, a circumstance that also would surely invite leaks.

It is not possible to reduce the difficult process of allied consultations to a set of propositions. But it is necessary to remember to manage the process carefully.

In the end, negotiations are worthwhile. At a minimum, they are likely to clear away misconceptions and improve the conditions for eventual improvements. So long as proceedings are undertaken carefully, without a sense of pressure, and with an eye fixed on the above cautions, even an unsuccessful effort need not be costly. And who knows, there might be success. The potential rewards in regional stability are great enough to warrant considerable efforts.

Chapter 4
The Iranian Nuclear Issue

Simon Shercliff

Goal: An Iran Without Nuclear Weapons

The Iranian nuclear issue has not been far from the top of the international agenda since late 2002, when important but hitherto secret aspects of the Iranian program were first brought to the attention of the general public. The issue is simple: whatever the reality of Iran's motivations, intentions, and scientific progress, there are fundamental reasons to be concerned about Iran's activities involving uranium enrichment and heavy water projects. The concern of the British government is that these proliferation-sensitive activities, like plutonium reprocessing, could become part of a nuclear weapons program.

The goal of the British government is to ensure that Iran does not build a nuclear weapon. London believes that the best way to do this is by securing an Iranian suspension of proliferation-sensitive nuclear activities until the international community can be satisfied that Iran's intentions are indeed peaceful, as the Iranians claim. The United Kingdom and its allies are not trying to stop Iran from constructing power reactors that will generate electricity as part of a peaceful, civilian nuclear program.

Why Are We Worried?

Our concern, shared formally with members of the International Atomic Energy Agency (IAEA) Board of Governors and the United Nations (UN) Security Council and informally with almost every other country in the world, is that the Iranian regime wants to acquire a nuclear weapons capability. This concern is rooted in the huge confidence deficit felt by the international community in Iran's intentions. This lack of confidence stems in large measure from the inability to understand Iran's urgent determination to develop uranium enrichment and heavy water projects for which it currently has no apparent civilian need, but which would give it the capabilities to produce fissile material for a nuclear weapon.

The Treaty on the Non-proliferation of Nuclear Weapons (NPT) does allow its nonnuclear-weapon state parties to develop sensitive fuel cycle technologies, but only if they are properly declared and safeguarded.[1] Iran has fallen short compared to other countries in this last regard. It has been found in past noncompliance with the treaty's safeguards obligations and has continued to be much less than fully cooperative with the IAEA. This is another major reason for the confidence deficit in Iran's intentions.

The international community has many questions about why Iran is in such a hurry to develop its enrichment program. Enrichment facilities are expensive, and most operators of civilian nuclear power stations contract their fuel supply from elsewhere for this reason, particularly if they only have a few power reactors. Iran has only one civilian nuclear power station, which is being built in Bushehr by the Russians. It is not yet completed. The Russians have guaranteed the fuel supply for the first ten years of Bushehr's operation, with the prospect of continued supply beyond that period. No one is trying to prevent the Russians from completing construction on the Bushehr plant or from supplying its fuel.

There are two other reasons for concern. First, prior to 2002, Iran deliberately concealed the proliferation-sensitive elements of its nuclear program for almost twenty years. It did so in clear contravention of its Comprehensive Safeguards Agreement with the IAEA under the NPT, and it has never been able to explain why.[2] Second, once the

---

1. Editor's Note: The Treaty on the Non-proliferation of Nuclear Weapons entered into force in 1970 and currently has 187 member states. The United Nations site has information about the treaty as well as the full text (http://www.un.org/Depts/dda/WMD/treaty/).

2. Editor's Note: According to the IAEA site, "Safeguards are activities by which the IAEA can verify that a State is living up to its international commitments not to use nuclear programs for nuclear-weapons purposes." See IAEA, "IAEA Safeguards Overview: Comprehensive Safeguards Agreements and Additional Protocols" (http://www.iaea.org/Publications/Factsheets/English/sg_overview.html).

IAEA inspectors were permitted into Iran, under great international pressure, to assess the hitherto secret aspects of Iran's nuclear program, they uncovered evidence that called into question Iran's activity relating to what the IAEA itself has called "possible military dimensions to Iran's nuclear program."[3] Iran is still refusing to answer these questions. These and other concerns create the confidence deficit that the international community feels about Iran's intentions.

The IAEA, in its report on Iran's nuclear program (19 November 2008), repeated its frustration that Iran is still not sufficiently cooperating.[4] Moreover, according to this report, Iran had almost 4,000 centrifuges being fed with uranium hexafluoride (UF6) gas, and all the indications are that it intends to install additional centrifuges.[5] The report showed that Iran has already enriched 630 kilograms of low enriched uranium (LEU). It also makes clear that Iran is still refusing to implement the Additional Protocol, which it has already signed.[6]

---

3. Editor's Note: See IAEA, "Implementation of the NPT Safeguards Agreement and Relevant Provisions of Security Council Resolutions 1737 (2006), 1747 (2007), 1803 (2008), and 1835 (2008) in the Islamic Republic of Iran," Report by the Director General, GOV/2008/59, 19 November 2008 (http://www.iaea.org/Publications/Documents/Board/2008/gov2008-59.pdf). See also that organization's site, "In Focus: IAEA and Iran," which includes an archive of reports, statements, and UN resolutions (http://www.iaea.org/NewsCenter/Focus/IaeaIran/index.shtml).

4. Editor's Note: See IAEA, "Implementation of the NPT Safeguards Agreement and Relevant Provisions of Security Council Resolutions 1737 (2006), 1747 (2007), 1803 (2008), and 1835 (2008) in the Islamic Republic of Iran," Report by the Director General, GOV/2008/59, 19 November 2008 (http://www.iaea.org/Publications/Documents/Board/2008/gov2008-59.pdf).

5. Editor's Note: According to a report issued by the IAEA director general "On 1 February 2009, 3936 centrifuges were being fed with UF6; 1476 centrifuges were installed and under vacuum, and an additional 125 centrifuges were installed but not under vacuum." See IAEA, "Implementation of the NPT Safeguards Agreement and Relevant Provisions of Security Council Resolutions 1737 (2006), 1747 (2007), 1803 (2008) and 1835 (2008) in the Islamic Republic of Iran," Report by the Director General, GOV/2009/8, 19 February 2009 (http://www.iaea.org/Publications/Documents/Board/2009/gov2009-8.pdf).

6. Editor's Note: According to the IAEA site, the Additional Protocol is a legal document complementing comprehensive safeguards agreements. The measures enable the IAEA not only to verify the non-diversion of declared nuclear material but also to provide assurances as to the absence of undeclared nuclear material and activities in a state. See IAEA, "IAEA Safeguards Overview: Comprehensive Safeguards Agreements and Additional Protocols" (http://www.iaea.org/Publications/Factsheets/English/sg_overview.html). For Iran's signing of the Additional Protocol on 18 December 2003, see the IAEA site (http://www.iaea.org/NewsCenter/News/2003/iranap20031218.html).

This lack of cooperation inevitably leads to the suspicion that Iran does not want to provide the IAEA with the greater information and access that an Additional Protocol would give compared to Iran's Comprehensive Safeguards Agreement with the agency.

The director general of the IAEA, Mohamed M. ElBaradei, observed in September 2008 that "only through the expeditious resolution of these outstanding issues can doubts arising there from about the exclusively peaceful nature of Iran's nuclear programme be dispelled, particularly in light of many years of clandestine activities by Iran."[7]

Notwithstanding its Obligations, What is the Problem with Iran Having a Nuclear Weapon?

Iran's development of a nuclear weapon would have dangerous consequences in an already unstable region. Iran might be emboldened to exert its influence even more than it is already doing. Other countries in the region would consider acquiring their own nuclear capabilities, driven by their own mistrust of Iran's intentions. Iranian possession of a nuclear weapon also could do great damage to regional security and to the NPT, which remains the cornerstone of the international nuclear nonproliferation regime.

What About Allowing Limited Enrichment on Iranian Soil, which They Seem to Want?

Many experts believe that if Iran is allowed to continue with developing uranium enrichment technology, even on a small scale, this experience would enable them to replicate the technology elsewhere in a covert military program.[8] It is worth noting that when the United Kingdom developed its own centrifuge enrichment program, it ran a sixteen-

---

7. Editor's Note: See IAEA, "Implementation of the NPT Safeguards Agreement and relevant provisions of Security Council resolutions 1737 (2006), 1747 (2007), and 1803 (2008) in the Islamic Republic of Iran," Report by the Director General, GOV/2008/38, 15 September 2008 (http://www.iaea.org/Publications/Documents/Board/2008/gov2008-38.pdf).

8. Editor's Note: For examples, see Patrick Clawson and Michael Eisenstadt, *The Last Resort: Consequences of Preventative Military Action against Iran*. Policy Focus, no. 84. (Washington D.C.: Washington Institute for Near East Policy, 2008; online at http://www.washingtoninstitute.org/pubPDFs/PolicyFocus84.pdf); and Kori Schake, "Dealing with a Nuclear Iran," *Policy Review* 142 (April and May 2007; online at http://www.hoover.org/publications/policyreview/6848072.html).

centrifuge cascade for two years before moving to larger cascades. It was this very limited program that allowed us to take significant steps toward mastering the processes and technology.

In addition, as has been pointed out by some experts, if Iran is permitted to continue small-scale enrichment, the IAEA would be hindered in its efforts to detect clandestine enrichment activity because procurement of the necessary materials for a clandestine program could be masked by legitimate procurement for the permitted program.[9]

Iran has already produced 630 kilograms of UF6 enriched to 3.5 percent LEU. Unless there is a suspension of its production soon, it may not be long before Iran has generated sufficient LEU to enable it to produce, after further enrichment, enough highly enriched uranium (HEU) for a first weapon. These developments reinforce the need for us to move fast toward our goal: regaining Iranian suspension of its program until we can be sure of its intentions.

So What Are We Doing About It?

In confronting this challenge, we are up against a self-confident, ideological regime. It senses that the West currently is overburdened in Iraq and Afghanistan and unwilling or unable to challenge Iran in a meaningful way. Until recently, with oil at $140-plus per barrel, it was flush with cash.[10] But Iran too is now suffering with the downturn in the international financial situation, and sanctions are biting. Our need is to present the Iranian decision-making machinery—confusing and opaque though it is—with an absolutely clear choice between cooperation and confrontation with the international community. The best policy is the classic diplomatic approach of carrots and sticks. This is the so-called dual-track policy, settled on and implemented by the UN Security Council at the instigation of the E3+3 (United Kingdom, United States, France, Germany, Russia, and China).

---

9. Ibid.

10. Editor's Note: This refers to oil prices in June-July 2008. See U.S. Department of Energy, Energy Information Agency, "Petroleum Navigator" (http://tonto.eia.doe.gov/dnav/pet/hist/wtotworldw.htm).

Iran does have a choice between confronting or cooperating. It is clear that some in the regime worry that the price of confrontation is too high. Others are interested in the benefits a good relationship with the international community can bring. We need to continue making plain this choice in order to achieve the eventual goal.

Why Do We Think Such an Approach Will Work?

First, some in the Iranian regime, unlike in Saddam Hussein's Iraq or Kim Jong-il's North Korea, want to be respectable. The regime goes to great lengths to present its nuclear program as legal. This means that censure by international organizations like the IAEA and UN Security Council, and the international unanimity we have worked hard to maintain through the E3+3, are powerful points of pressure in their own right.

Second, Iran, while far from being an ideal democracy, does have a system that allows for some differences of opinion and in which there are competing voices and power centers. There is, therefore, considerable debate within the country on the regime's handling of the nuclear file, often in public, and there may be opportunities to exploit this debate to our advantage.

Third, Iran has a young, open society, and the majority of its people aspire to reintegrate with the world. This offers us the opportunities through our policies to influence political debates and create bottom-up pressures.

Fourth, we have things that Iran needs, including the technology that it needs to develop and meet the needs of its young population.

How Does the Policy Work?

Sustained, unanimous diplomatic pressure is one powerful tool at our disposal. Iran has consistently and incorrectly calculated that it can divide the international community. It thought that China and Russia would never allow them to be referred to the UN Security Council.

Once there, they thought that China and Russia would never allow the adoption of sanctions against them. In fact, the Security Council has now adopted five mandatory resolutions on Iran.[11]

Sanctions and economic pressures are another important tool. They affect the debate at different levels. Ordinary Iranians worry about the impact of inflation and growing unemployment. The financial sector is suffering from financial sanctions. The politically influential *bazaari* (merchant) class are finding it increasingly expensive and difficult to do business as access to international credit dries up. Many European banks have stopped dealing with Iran. In the United Kingdom, for example, Iranian banks no longer have access to clearance in sterling.

Finally, we see real nervousness about the impact of de facto sanctions. Iran's aging oil industry is creaking, with production declining. The future depends on the development of Iran's enormous gas reserves, but to do so will require both technology and major foreign investment. The political class and technocrats worry about how Iran is going to pay the bills and provide for its people, 70 percent of whom are under age thirty, in a few years' time.

So while we have not yet persuaded them to stop enriching, pressures are building. The European Union (EU) has already applied measures complementary to, and exceeding, UN Security Council Resolution (UNSCR) 1803.[12] Measures that both processes have so far yielded include: designating banks; making further travel bans and asset freezes; limiting export credits; imposing export bans on sensitive dual-use items; and conducting cargo inspections for Iran's national airline and shipping line. But we must still do more, and do it urgently.

---

11. Editor's Note: Four UNSCR resolutions were adopted unanimously: 1737 (2006); 1747 (2007); 1803 (2008); 1835 (2008). A fifth, 1696 (2006) was passed with a vote of fourteen in favor, and one (Qatar) opposed. All of the resolutions can be found online through both the UN (http://www.un.org/documents/scres.htm) and the IAEA (http://www.iaea.org/NewsCenter/Focus/IaeaIran/index.shtml).

12. Editor's Note: UNSCR 1803 (March 2008) called for Iran to abide by the NPT (http://www.iaea.org/NewsCenter/Focus/IaeaIran/unsc_res1803-2008.pdf).

While increasing pressure is important, the other strand of our policy is the carrots. Sharpening the choice for Iranian decision-makers means demonstrating that there is a price to be paid for unacceptable policies, but also that there is a way out if the regime modifies its behavior. That means continuing to hold out the offer of a new relationship if Iran modifies its policies. The package that the E3+3 first proposed in June 2006—with the U.S. administration's support—remains on the table and was "refreshed" in June 2008. This offer includes providing help to Iran to build power reactors for the generation of electricity and guaranteeing supplies of nuclear fuel for them. It also would extend significant political and economic benefits, including a trade and cooperation agreement and strategic energy partnership with the EU, the lifting of sanctions in some areas crucial to the Iranian economy, and the chance to discuss regional security issues with the six as a whole, including the United States.

Conclusion

Our approach should remain one of using a combination of pressure and incentives to persuade the Iranians to change their behavior. There are always frustrations with such an approach, but we believe that, if vigorously pursued, this approach can still offer the best way of achieving our ultimate goal: an Iran without nuclear weapons.

Chapter 5
Reflections on Iran's Policy Toward Iraq
Mohsen M. Milani

There are hardly any disagreements among experts that the Islamic Republic of Iran is an influential and important foreign power in post-Saddam Hussein Iraq. At dispute is the extent of that power as well as Iran's intentions and objectives. On one hand, there are those who maintain that Iraq is "lost" to Iran. Saudi Arabia's foreign minister, Saud al-Faisal, was quoted in 2006 as saying that "we are handing the whole country [Iraq] to Iran without reason."[1] A 2007 report by the British Chatham House concluded that "Iran has superseded the U.S. as the most influential power in Iraq."[2] On the other hand, the Islamic Republic of Iran insists that Iran is well-intentioned and a natural ally of the new Iraq and that Iranian policy toward that country is designed solely to support the territorial integrity of Iraq and its political independence and economic prosperity. Tehran rejects as propaganda the assertion that it interferes in Iraq's internal affairs.

Although both of these extreme perspectives contain elements of truth, neither does justice in accurately depicting Iran's strategic goals or its actual power inside Iraq. This chapter briefly identifies some of Iran's main strategic goals toward the new Iraq without discussing the mechanisms, the tactics, and the channels Tehran is employing to achieve them. First, though, here are a few general comments about the nature of Iran's regional policies, placing Iran's policy toward Iraq in a proper context and framework.

---

1. Saud al-Faisal quoted in Megan K. Stack and Borzou Daragahi, "Iran Was on Edge; Now It's on Top," *Los Angeles Times*, 18 February 2006 (http://articles.latimes.com/2006/feb/18/world/fg-iranrising18).

2. Gareth R.V. Stansfield, "Accepting Realities in Iraq" (briefing paper, Chatham House, London, 2007), 8 (http://www.chathamhouse.org.uk/publications/papers/view/-/id/501/).

I. Is Iranian Foreign Policy Made by "Mad Mullahs" or by Calculating Ayatollahs?

In politics, perception is sometimes more powerful than reality. Incorrect perceptions can lead to incorrect policies, and misleading policies can have devastating consequences. For the past few years, a popular image has gained increasing acceptance in the American mass media and even among some prominent academics. This perception is labeled the "mad mullah narrative" in this article. Stripped to its core, the narrative depicts Iranian leaders as dangerously irrational and even suicidal, a cabal of mostly bearded and turbaned men who cannot be deterred and who are obsessed with apocalyptic delusions, imperial ambitions, and even harboring death wishes. Professor Bernard Lewis, an erudite historian of the Near East, portrays Iran's leaders as apocalyptic believers in martyrdom: "For people with this mindset, MAD [Mutually Assured Destruction] is not a constraint; it is an inducement."[3] Many others have embellished Lewis's alarmist assertions.[4] Norman Podhoretz, for example, argued that "if the mullahs get the bomb . . . it was not they who would be deterred, but we," because Iran's "Islamofascist revolutionaries" are "ready to die for their beliefs" and thus do not care "about protecting their people."[5]

Iranian President Mahmud Ahmadinejad's puerile questioning of the Holocaust, his reprehensive declaration that Israel "will be wiped out from the map of the world," and his policy of continuing to enrich

---

3. Bernard Lewis, "Does Iran Have Something in Store," *Wall Street Journal,* 8 August 2006 (http://www.opinionjournal.com/extra/?id=110008768).

4. See Christopher Orlet, "Apocalyptic Ahmadinejad," *American Spectator,* 6 October 2006 (http://spectator.org/archives/2006/10/06/apocalyptic-ahmadinejad); Walter R. Newell, "Why is Ahmadinejad Smiling? The Intellectual Sources of his Apocalyptic Vision," *Weekly Standard,* 16 November 2006 (http://www.weeklystandard.com/Content/Public/Articles/000/000/012/795hlmvk.asp); and Joel C. Rosenberg, "Apocalypse Now? Is Iran Planning a Cataclysmic Strike for August 22?" *National Review Online,* 10 August 2006 (http://article.nationalreview.com/?q=NWNmMWM5MjhhMzVjZTM0ZmI1ZmJlYzAxNzU3NDEyMWI=).

5. Norman Podhoretz, "Stopping Iran: Why the Case for Military Action Still Stands," *Commentary Magazine,* February 2008, 11-19 (http://www.commentarymagazine.com/viewpdf.cfm?article_id=11085).

uranium have surely rendered the mad mullah narrative deliciously palatable in the United States. But does the narrative accurately explain how key foreign policy decisions are made in Tehran?

The mad mullah narrative can unquestionably mobilize American public opinion against Iran's nuclear ambitions and could be used to justify "regime change" or even war with Iran. It also creates the unambiguous impression that negotiations with Tehran's "mad men" would be futile. Despite its clear benefits as a public relations strategy to undermine the Islamic Republic, the narrative's analytical utility is limited. First, it overexaggerates the impact of certain Shiite beliefs on Iranian policies and sometimes confuses the rhetorical pronouncements of Iranian leaders with their actual policies. Second, the narrative focuses mostly on Ahmadinejad's religious proclivities and creates the misleading impression that he, rather than Iran's supreme leader, Ayatollah Sayyed Ali Hoseyni Khamenei, is the ultimate "decider" of Iranian foreign policy.[6]

In Iran's bifurcated system of governance, the popularly elected president is a powerful force that cannot be ignored, but ultimately, he does not determine the tenor and direction of Iran's foreign and security policies. The supreme leader alone makes those vital decisions. Moreover, the supreme leader, and not the president, is the commander in chief of the Iranian armed forces, including the regular armed forces and the Pasdaran (Islamic Revolution Guard Corps [IRGC]). The supreme leader appoints all commanders of Iran's military and paramilitary forces. All report directly to him, and all are accountable to him, not to the president.

The supreme leader, who is unquestionably the most powerful figure in the Islamic Republic, does not run a one-man show, however, as Iran's last monarch did. Despite all his powers, the supreme leader must operate in a complex, fluid, and unpredictable system. To secure his own position, he must maintain some semblance of neutrality in a

---

6. For an analysis of the role and ideas of Khamenei, see Karim Sadjadpour, *Reading Khamenei: The World View of Iran's Most Powerful Leader* (Washington D.C.: Carnegie Endowment for International Peace, 2008), as well as Sadjadpour's essay in this book (chapter 2).

highly factionalized polity, address the needs of various interest groups, and appease ambitious politicians and clerics.[7] His most important responsibility is in fact protecting the survival of the entire system.

The mad mullah narrative seems to put the cart in front of the horse: Iranian policy makers formulate policy only after they determine their goals, evaluate their resources, and assess their enemies. Only then do they open their diverse ideological/Islamic toolbox to choose the most appropriate religious beliefs or symbols to legitimize and ultimately achieve their desired goals. The mad mullah narrative thus has the order in reverse. By focusing strictly on the religious dimension of Iranian foreign policy, the advocates of the mad mullah narrative are destined to see the tree but miss the forest.

Most critically, the mad mullah narrative ignores that both regime survival and expediency have played an infinitely more defining role in Iran's foreign policies than some of its leaders' apocalyptic and messianic beliefs. With the 1979 Tehran hostage crisis, former allies Iran and the United States became bitter enemies. Since that time, Iran's top leadership, from Ayatollah Ruhollah Musavi Khomeini to Ayatollah Khamenei, has consistently perceived the United States as an existential threat.[8] Ironically, both the shah's regime and the Islamic Republic relied on an "American-centric" foreign policy to survive: the former by its alliance with the United States, and the latter by its unremitting hostility toward America.

Obsessed with regime survival, Iranian leaders have also skillfully institutionalized *maslehat*, or expediency. In the convoluted vernacular of Iranian foreign policy, *maslehat* can be accurately interpreted as nothing less than a "cost-benefit" approach to decision making. Interestingly, the 2007 U.S. National Intelligence Estimate (NIE), "Iran: Nuclear Intentions and Capabilities," profoundly debunked

---

7. Mehran Kamrava and Houchang Hassan-Yari offer an interesting analysis of the inner workings of Iran's factionalized system. See their "Suspended Equilibrium in Iran's Political System," *The Muslim World* 94 (October 2004): 495-524.

8. See Barbara Slavin, *Bitter Friends, Bosom Enemies: Iran, the U.S., and the Twisted Path to Confrontation* (New York: St. Martin's Press, 2007).

the key assumptions of the mad mullah narrative; instead, it offered a nuanced and more accurate picture of how decisions are made in Iran.[9] Based on the consensus of sixteen intelligence agencies, the controversial report concluded that Iran halted its "nuclear weapons program" in 2003 based on a "cost-benefit" approach—the exact opposite of what the mad mullah narrative suggests. Thus the report recognizes that Iran is not run by mad mullahs, but rather by calculating ayatollahs. There are in fact numerous other cases in which the Islamic Republic has utilized a "cost-benefit" approach in making key foreign policy decisions.

During the hostage crisis (1979-81), Khomeini ordered the release of the hostages only after the benefits outweighed the costs.[10] The same "cost-benefit" approach guided his decision in approving secret dealings with the United States and Israel, which he had called the "Great Satan" and "Smaller Satan," respectively. His tactical goal was to obtain weapons in order to achieve the strategic objective of defeating Iraq on the battlefield. Equally telling was the pivotal moment when he faced the impossibility of victory and the growing domestic opposition to the war Saddam Hussein had started and he had refused to end: Khomeini said he was willing to drink "from the chalice of poison" in order to sanction a cease-fire with Iraq in 1988. He justified it as *maslehat*.

The same temperament of decision making continued after Khomeini's death. During the Persian Gulf War in 1991, Tehran retained active neutrality, although Saddam Hussein offered lucrative concessions in an attempt to woo Tehran to side with him. Tehran also welcomed the liberation of Kuwait, acquiesced to the presence of U.S. troops in the region, and remained silent when Saddam massacred Iraqi Shiites. Those decisions were made because the new president, Ali Akbar Hashemi Rafsanjani, and the new supreme leader, Khamenei, did not

---

9. National Intelligence Council, "Iran: Nuclear Intentions and Capabilities" (National Intelligence Estimate, November 2007; online at http://www.dni.gov/press_releases/20071203_release.pdf).

10. See Mohsen M. Milani, "The Hostage Crisis," *Encyclopedia Iranica* (New York: Columbia University Press, 2004; online at http://www.iranica.com/newsite/).

wish to antagonize the West in the unpredictable environment of the post-Khomeini era. Their ultimate goal was to consolidate their power.

Most interestingly, Iran did not support the Republic of Azerbaijan, the only country besides Iran and Iraq that is predominantly Shiite, in its conflict against the Republic of Armenia, an orthodox Christian country (1988-94). Iran's motivation was, and still is, to protect its province of Azerbaijan against any secessionist impulse supported by the Republic of Azerbaijan. Similarly, Tehran did not back the Muslim Chechens against predominantly Christian Russia, whose support Iran needed to neutralize the U.S. containment of the Islamic Republic.

Iran's strategies changed after the United States toppled the Taliban in 2001.[11] In Afghanistan, the IRGC rubbed shoulders with U.S. military advisors, providing intelligence to assist in the defeat of the Taliban. At the same time, Iran moved opportunistically to gain strategic depth by expanding its sphere of influence in that country.

In all the cases cited above, decisions were made after a deliberative process; in each instance, the traits of flexibility were apparent. It would be foolhardy to think that the Iranian leadership formulates its foreign or nuclear policies based on such notions as the return of the Imam or martyrdom. Such beliefs are central to Shiite consciousness, but they cannot alone explain Iranian policies. The track record of the Islamic Republic in the past thirty years similarly does not suggest that the ayatollahs are suicidal, even if they support gullible masses who commit suicidal acts, and even though Iran has sponsored terrorism in some aspects of its foreign policy.

General John P. Abizaid, former commander of U.S. Central Command, understands these realities about the leadership of the Islamic Republic. He argues that while everything must be done to prevent Iran from going nuclear, the United States is perfectly capable

---

11. See Mohsen M. Milani, "Iran's Policy Toward Afghanistan," *Middle East Journal* 60 (Spring 2006): 235-56.

of containing a nuclear Iran, just as it contained the Soviet Union.[12] Similar to the NIE, General Abizaid rejects the notion that Iranian leaders are irrational or suicidal. The political ramifications of such conclusions are rather straightforward: you can negotiate with Iran even though you might despise the regime and its policies.

II. Iran's Top Strategic Goals in Iraq

It is gradually becoming conventional wisdom in Washington that Iran has emerged as a regional power in one of the most troubled and strategically vital regions of the world. In an article published in 2005, I made the same argument and maintained that Iranian policy toward Iraq needs to be analyzed and understood in the framework of Iran's emergence as a regional player.[13] By removing the Taliban and Saddam Hussein from power—Iran's two nemeses—the United States accelerated Iran's drive toward being a regional power, a process that began some years ago.[14] Today, the United States and Iran are engaged in a fierce rivalry within Central Asia, the Caucuses, and a vast area between Afghanistan and Lebanon. That competition shapes the direction of Iranian foreign policy in fundamental ways.

Mohsen Rezai, a former IRGC commander, reflects the dominant view of the foreign policy establishment in Tehran when he argues that Iran is an "indispensable" regional power. He wrote in 2007:

> Today Iran has no meaning without Iraq, Lebanon, Palestine, and Syria. There was a time when Iran within its [own] borders meant something, but today, Iran is the region and our identity has now become intertwined with that of the region. It is our principle and undisputable right to become a regional

---

12. David E. Sanger and Thom Shanker, "Washington Sees an Opportunity in Iranian's Defiance," *New York Times*, 27 September 2007 (http://query.nytimes.com/gst/fullpage.htm l?res=9E03E0DE1E3EF934A1575AC0A9619C8B63&sec=&spon=&&scp=1&sq=Washing ton%20Sees%20an%20Opportunity%20in%20Iranian%E2%80%99s%20Defiance&st=cse).
13. Mohsen M. Milani, "Iran, the Status Quo Power," *Current History*, January 2005, 30-36.
14. Ibid.

power. We are a nation that can play such a leadership role, but they [the West/U.S.] would like to deprive us from playing such a role.[15]

The administration of U.S. President George W. Bush seemed to partially agree with Rezai's analysis. In discussing the passage of United Nations Security Council Resolution (UNSCR) 1747 in March of 2007, a U.S. official confirmed that the imposed sanctions had broader goals than just dealing with Iran's nuclear program: "Its language was written to rein in what they [Security Council members] see as Tehran's ambitions to become the dominant military power in the Persian Gulf and across the broader Middle East."[16]

It is only after Iran is viewed as an emerging regional power with its own set of priorities and objectives that an understanding of the complexities of Iran's deep involvement in Iraq today can take place.[17] The remainder of this article briefly discusses five of Iran's goals in Iraq. This list is far from complete and omits some key components of Iranian policy. It also does not address the nature of Iran's support, military or otherwise, to various groups inside Iraq, nor the complex economic and security relations with Iraq; nor does this list address Iranian involvement in the Attabat (the cities in southern Iraq where the shrines of Shiite imams are located and a considerable population of Iranians or Iraqis of Iranian descent reside). However, this list is useful in understanding the overall themes of Iranian policy in Iraq and may serve as guidelines for future policy makers.

The list of five goals is not based on the order of their significance or their priority for Tehran, partly because Iranian policy toward Iraq changes as the ground situation in Iraq changes. Moreover, Iranian

---

15. Iranian Students News Agency, 26 February 2007, translation by the author (http://www.isna.ir/).

16. Thom Shanker, "Security Council Votes to Tighten Iran Sanctions," *New York Times*, 25 March 2007 (http://www.nytimes.com/2007/03/25/world/middleeast/25sanctions.html?_r=1&scp=1&sq=Security%20Council%20Votes%20to%20Tighten%20Iran%20Sanctions&st=cse).

17. The main arguments in this section are taken from my forthcoming book chapter, "Iran's Persian Gulf Policy in the Post-Saddam Era," in Ali Gheissari, ed., *Contemporary Iran: Economy, Society, Politics* (New York: Oxford University Press, 2009).

policy toward Iraq is organically linked to Iran's regional policies and to its own security concerns. Chief among these concerns are the situations in Afghanistan and Lebanon; the Arab-Israeli conflict; Iran's nuclear dispute with the West; and Tehran's perceived threat from Washington. In short, an Iran that believes it is making progress on these key fronts is an Iran that is more likely to collaborate with the United States in Iraq. An Iran whose survival is perceived as threatened, and whose security needs and growing regional influence are both ignored and not respected, is an Iran that is more likely to involve itself in acts of mischief against the United States in Iraq.

In Iraq, as elsewhere, Iranian policy is determined by the "cost-benefit" approach. Iran's first and most important strategic goal toward Iraq is to ensure that a friendly Shiite-dominated government remains in power in Baghdad. Iran's preference seems to be a reasonably strong federal system—powerful enough to impose internal order and maintain cohesion, but not strong enough to pose a serious security threat to the Islamic Republic. Iran understands that demography in elections is destiny and has consistently called for and supported free national elections in Iraq, convinced that the Shiite majority will prevail. Both Washington and Tehran have thus far supported successive Iraqi governments in the post-Saddam era; thus, there seems to be a convergence of strategic interests between them. Among Iraq's neighbors, and in fact among all Islamic countries, none has been as supportive of the post-Saddam governments in Iraq as Iran has.

There are both strategic and security-related reasons for Iranian support for establishing a friendly Iraqi government in Baghdad. Iranian engagement in Iraq has deep historical roots that predate the advent of Islam. Ctesiphon, one of the palaces of the Sassanid dynasty (226-642), was located in the vicinity of present-day Baghdad. In the Islamic period, Persians provided financial and logistical support to the Abbasids, who overthrew the Ummayd dynasty (661-750) and moved the capital of the Islamic empire from Damascus to Baghdad. The era universally recognized as the golden age of Islam during the Abbasid rule was greatly aided by great Persian thinkers: scientists like Abu

Bakr Muhammad ibn Zakariya Razi, who discovered how to make alcohol (ethanol); Avicenna (Ibn Sina), who is known as the prince of physicians; and mathematicians like Abu Abdallah Muhammad ibn Musa al-Khwarizmi, who was one of the fathers of algebra.

Iran continued to play an important role in Mesopotamia when it was part of the Ottoman Empire. For nearly four centuries, until the British established Iraq in 1921, the Persian Empire, as the defender of the Shiite faith, and the Ottoman Empire, as the protector of Sunni faith, fought numerous wars and signed more than twenty bilateral agreements about the thorny issue of the control over Mesopotamia. Historically, Iranian strategists looked at Mesopotamia and later Iraq as a prized and key region to expand Iranian influence in the Middle East as well as a dangerous land bridge for cruel invaders.

There is simply no other issue more important to Tehran than preventing the establishment of an Iraqi government that is hostile to Iran, be it Shiite- or Sunni-dominated. This is indeed the defining lesson Iran has learned from its bloody, long, and devastating war with Iraq—a war that Saddam Hussein started. Not since the Twelver Shiism was established as the state religion in Iran in 1501 has any country inflicted as much pain, suffering, and destruction on Iran as did Iraq during the Iran-Iraq War of 1980 to 1988. This explains why, when the U.S. troops overthrew Saddam Hussein, Iranians from all walks of life celebrated the historic event, some privately and many publicly. The Iranian policy of supporting a friendly government in Iraq, therefore, has a popular base of support within Iran. Tehran is likely to support any Shiite government, even a highly secular one, as long as it is not overtly hostile to Iran.

Iran's second goal, which is in many ways complementary to its first, is the empowerment of the Shiite groups. Tehran has pursued this goal with sensitivity, determined not to alienate the Sunnis and certainly not the Kurds. The clerical leadership in Tehran views the Iraqi Shiites as a natural ally and sees their empowerment as a vehicle that would facilitate the expansion of Iranian influence within Iraq, the Persian

Gulf, and far beyond. Tehran believes that the situation in Iraq is still fluid and that Iraq is in the first phase of a dangerous transition whose outcome is rather uncertain and hard to predict. To be on the winning side, therefore, Tehran is hedging its bets, supporting all Shiite factions, albeit to different degrees, and is seeking not to alienate any such group.

This is not to suggest that Tehran's real agenda is to establish an Iranian-style Islamic order in Iraq—far from that. Iran understands that the Sunni minority as well as the Kurds would vociferously and violently reject such a Shiite theocracy. In the event of a partitioning of Iraq along sectarian lines, this policy can of course change, and Iran would then likely support an Iranian-style government in what could become a new "Shiistan."

Iranian support for the main Shiite groups predates the removal of Saddam Hussein. During the Iran-Iraq War, Iran helped create the Supreme Council for the Islamic Revolution in Iraq (SCIRI) and trained its military wing, the Badr Brigade.[18] Tehran also supported the Al-Dawa Party.[19] Those two organizations have been the most powerful forces within the successive Iraqi governments since Saddam Hussein was overthrown. Additionally, they are Iran's most trusted allies. To this day, Iran has maintained close and friendly relations with both and has sought to manage and contain tensions and disagreements with them, particularly over the issue of the future role of the United States in Iraq and the two organizations' intimate connection to the U.S.

The Shiites of Iraq are hardly homogenous and are divided along ideological and class lines. Iran is expanding its influence among all of

---

18. Editor's Note: The Supreme Council for the Islamic Revolution in Iraq (SCIRI) is an Iraqi Shiite political party founded in 1982 and is supported by Iran. The SCIRI adheres to the tenets of Khomeini's velayat-e faqih. See Kenneth Katzman, "Iran's Activities and Influence in Iraq" (Congressional Research Service report for Congress, 8 November 2007; online at http://fpc.state.gov/documents/organization/96430.pdf).

19. Editor's Note: Al-Dawa party is an Iraqi Shiite political party that supported the Islamic Revolution in Iran and opposed Saddam Hussein. It continues to receive support from Tehran and are part of the "United Iraqi Alliance," a Shiite Islamist bloc. See ibid.

them. This explains the Iranian support for the rebel cleric, Muqtada al-Sadr, and his Mahdi Army.[20] Iran has supported Sadr not so much because it endorses and appreciates his nationalistic and anti-Persian sentiments, but because he can provide insurance for Tehran in case Tehran's two favorite organizations alluded to earlier were to fail. Moreover, al-Sadr's movement is popular among the lower-class Shiites, particularly in Baghdad, and Tehran cannot afford to not support them. Tehran also views al-Sadr as a potential counterforce against the more moderate clerics, particularly Grand Ayatollah Ali al-Husayni al-Sistani, whose views on *velayat-e faqih*, the philosophical underpinning of Iran's system of governance, are radically different from Iran's governing ayatollahs. Finally, Tehran has supported Sadr because his insurgency opposed U.S. occupation and undermined the American presence in Iraq.

Iran's third goal is to reduce U.S. influence in Iraq and prevent the United States from establishing permanent military bases in Iraq. This goal is probably the most complex of all of Iran's objectives, and its nature has changed over time. At first, the remarkably easy U.S. victory in Iraq frightened the ayatollahs who thought Iran, as a certified member of the "Axis of Evil," might be the next target of American wrath. That initial fear dissipated as the Iraqi insurgency gained momentum, however, and Tehran came to the conclusion that a U.S. invasion of Iran is no longer feasible. For years now, Tehran appears to have made an important strategic decision to avoid any direct military confrontation with the United States. This does not mean or imply that Iran has not actively sought to undermine the Americans in Iraq. It surely has. It is clear that Tehran's policy has oscillated between the two goals of preventing the U.S. from a total and clean victory and of avoiding any direct confrontation with the United States.

Iran's fourth goal is to expand its sphere of influence in southern Iraq. Just as Iran has created a sphere of influence in Herat Province in

---

20. Editor's Note: The Mahdi Army is an Iraqi Shiite paramilitary force that has opposed the Coalition presence within post-Saddam Hussein Iraq. Created in 2003 by Muqtada al-Sadr, this group has received support from Tehran. See Ibid.

western Afghanistan, it would like to expand its power in southern Iraq. Iran's rather extensive participation in Iraq's reconstruction, particularly in the Shiite-dominated areas, is part and parcel of this policy.

The creation of spheres of influence, which include support for formal and informal organizations, is a central component of Iran's deterrence strategy as well as a function of both its ambitions and its threat perceptions. It is designed to deter potential aggression, to bolster Iran's regional standing, and to protect its interests. There is also an economic dimension to this strategy: Iran seeks to become a hub for the transit of goods and services between the Persian Gulf, Iraq, Afghanistan, Central Asia, and possibly China.

Iran's fifth goal is to help maintain the territorial integrity of Iraq and to thus prevent its Balkanization. Iran, like Turkey, would not tolerate an autonomous Kurdistan in Iraq. The creation of an independent Kurdistan could entice Iran's other ethnic minorities to establish their own autonomous governments. This, in turn, would jeopardize Iran's own territorial integrity.

Iran is also concerned about two other key issues. One of these sources of anxiety is the possible manipulation of the Iraqi-based *Mojahedin-e Khalq* (MEK) to destabilize Iran. That organization was supported by Saddam Hussein and operated within Iraq; its members are now under direct American control.[21] Tehran, like the United States, considers this organization a terrorist entity. However, Tehran condemns the U.S. failure to condemn and disarm the MEK and believes that MEK members can be trained to destabilize Iran.

Iran also worries about the potential for U.S. manipulation of the Qom-Najaf corridor. Historically, the seminaries, or *hawzeh*, in Iraq

---

21. Editor's Note: The main MEK base is Camp Ashraf. According to Acting Deputy Department Spokesman Gordon Duguid of the U.S. State Department, "the disposition of Camp Ashraf was given a full transfer to the responsibility of the Iraqis on February the 20th [2009]." He went on to say, "responsibility for resolving the situation at the camp rests with the Government of Iraq at this time." For full statement, see the Daily Press Briefing, 30 March 2009 (http://www.state.gov/r/pa/prs/dpb/2009/03/120983.htm). See also Abigail Hauslohner, "Iranian Group a Source of Contention in Iraq," *Time*, 5 January 2009 (http://www.time.com/time/world/article/0,8599,1869532,00.html).

have had a significant impact on Iranian politics. Today, there are those in Iran, including some clerics, who either seek to democratize or altogether reject the *velayat-e faqih* doctrine. These voices are often suppressed. A powerful *hawzeh* in Najaf could reverse this trend. Ayatollah Sistani, who has millions of followers in Iran, belongs to the "quietist" school of Shiite thought, which rejects Khomeini's interpretation of the *velayat-e faqih* doctrine. Could a Najaf *hawzeh* that is unfriendly toward Iran's version of the *velayat-e faqih* doctrine and is supported with Iraqi petrodollars pose a significant threat to the durability of Iran's clerical government?

It appears that Iran enjoys more power in Iraq than the other neighbors of Iraq. Still, its power is rather limited, and it is unable to determine the future of Iraq, although it can become a spoiler and disrupt any Western design for Iraq. Additionally, Iraqi Shiites, who are Iran's main lever of influence in Iraq, are first and foremost Iraqis and thus will not allow Iraq to become anything more than an ally of Iran—and certainly not a proxy.

Today, Iran has clear security concerns and identifiable interests in Iraq. The United States could simply ignore Iran and seek to marginalize it. This path would likely lead to more instability in Iraq and the Persian Gulf. Alternatively, the two countries could recognize each other's interests and concerns and negotiate.[22] The fact that the two countries have held a few meetings at the ambassadorial level in Iraq is a small but prudent step in the right direction.

---

22. For further reading on negotiations, see the Karim Sadjadpour and Ronald E. Neumann essays in this book (chapters 2 and 3).

Chapter 6
Iran in the Israeli Threat Perception

Gerald M. Steinberg

Since independence in 1948, Israel has been faced with a complex security environment resulting from the combination of intense hostility and extreme asymmetry. Israel's territory is very narrow, with essentially no strategic depth. Strong and consistent responses to attack, including asymmetrical warfare and terror campaigns, have created a credible deterrent, contributed to the peace treaties with Egypt (1979) and Jordan (1994), and prevented direct clashes with Syria (since 1982).[1]

In parallel, however, the radius of the conflict has expanded far beyond the bordering Arab states, and the Islamic regime in Iran has become the main threat to Israeli security and regional stability. Although Israeli relations with Iran were quite cooperative until the Islamic revolution in 1979 and included significant strategic cooperation, this situation has changed completely in the last three decades.[2] Iran is now seen as a triumphalist force with steadily increasing influence and in the process of acquiring regional dominance, particularly following the 2003 war in Iraq that removed Saddam Hussein from power.

The Iranian threat takes many forms, including the Shiite Hezbollah force in Lebanon, which launched an attack in July 2006, and which is armed, trained, and financed from Tehran; the Hamas organization that controls Gaza fired thousands of rockets of increasing range at Israel until the December 2008 Israeli response; the Iranian alliance with Syria, which has provided support for ballistic missile

---

1. Gerald M. Steinberg, "Israel at Sixty: Asymmetry, Vulnerability, and the Search for Security" (Jerusalem Viewpoints 564, Jerusalem Center for Public Affairs, June 2008; online at http://www.jcpa.org/JCPA/Templates/ShowPage.asp?DBID=1&LNGID=1&TMID=111&FID=283&PID=1844&IID=2206).

2. David Menashri, "Iran, Israel and the Middle East Conflict," *Israel Affairs* 12 (January 2006): 107-22; Menashri, *Post-Revolutionary Politics in Iran: Religion, Society and Power* (London: Frank Cass, 2001).

development and may have been linked to the illicit North Korean nuclear reactor that was destroyed by Israel in September 2007; and the Iranian nuclear weapons project and ballistic missile capabilities.[3]

Iranian rhetoric and statements from leaders that reflect hatred and deny Israeli legitimacy, reinforced by military parades in Tehran featuring missiles with signs proclaiming "Wipe Israel off the Map" and "Destination Tel Aviv," increase the Israeli determination to prevent Iran from acquiring nuclear weapons. Iranian President Mahmud Ahmadinejad's genocidal declarations reflect a fundamentalist and apocalyptic Islamist whose words and intentions are focused on the destruction of Israel. The Holocaust denial conference that took place in early 2007 in Tehran, in which Ahmadinejad played a central role, highlighted the anti-Israeli rhetoric that has been part of the Islamic regime's platform from the beginning. In 2001, former President Ali Akbar Hashemi Rafsanjani called the establishment of Israel the "worst event in history" and declared that "in due time the Islamic world will have a military nuclear device, and then the strategy of the West would reach a dead end, since one bomb is enough to destroy all Israel."[4] Similar attention was given to bellicose statements by Iran's supreme leader, Ayatollah Sayyed Ali Hoseyni Khamenei, such as "the cancerous tumor called Israel must be uprooted."[5] Such statements provided evidence of the *intention*, while the pursuit of nuclear

---

3. Editor's Note: For more on the 2006 Lebanon war and the 2008 Gaza war, see Asher Susser, "The War in Gaza—A View from Israel" (Royal United Services Institute commentary, 13 January 2009; online at http://www.rusi.org/research/studies/menap/commentary/ref:C496C7AEB68B4A/); and Alon Ben-Meir, "After Gaza—A Two State Solution is the Only Option" (Royal United Services Institute commentary, 26 January 2009; online at http://www.rusi.org/research/studies/africa/commentary/ref:C497D9F21ECFCD/).

4. The Iranian broadcast agency released two versions of Rafsanjani's remarks, which were made during a Friday sermon (on "Quds," or Jerusalem Day) at a mosque on the campus of Tehran University. See "Qods Day Speech (Jerusalem Day): Chairman of Expediency Council Akbar Hashemi-Rafsanjani," Tehran, Voice of the Islamic Republic of Iran Radio 1, 14 December 2001 (http://www.globalsecurity.org/wmd/library/news/iran/2001/011214-text.html); "Iran: Expediency Council Office Says Israel Distorted its Chairman's Remarks," 2002 BBC Monitoring International Reports, 2 January 2002 (www.lexisnexis.com).

5. "Iran Leader Urges Destruction of 'Cancerous' Israel," Reuters, 15 December 2000 (http://archives.cnn.com/2000/WORLD/meast/12/15/mideast.iran.reut/).

weapons and ballistic missile delivery systems were the evidence of incipient *capability*.[6]

As a result, the question of how best to respond to the Iranian threat has become the central issue on the Israeli security agenda and also in the domestic political framework. Headlines in newspapers frequently highlight the latest Iranian developments, including weapons tests, exercises, and bellicose pronouncements. Israeli news, talk shows on radio and television, and academic conferences include frequent discussions and debates on the implications of the Iranian nuclear threat and potential policy options for response.[7] Sanctions, a preemptive military strike, deterrence, missile defense, and the likelihood that Egypt, Syria, Turkey, Algeria, and Saudi Arabia will follow Iran on the path to proliferation are among the topics.

International negotiations, very limited and belated sanctions, and the International Atomic Energy Agency (IAEA) inspection process under the Treaty on the Non-Proliferation of Nuclear Weapons (NPT) have failed to slow or end the Iranian nuclear program. The weakness of the United States in leading the international response, inept European diplomacy, and the hesitation of Russia and China have contributed to this outcome. Russia and China in particular have emphasized their competition with the United States over threats to their vital interests resulting from an Iranian nuclear capability. These slow-moving international responses have given the Iranian leaders the time necessary to expand their uranium enrichment and plutonium production efforts. The strategy of buying time has been very successful—from the Iranian perspective.

---

6. Ephraim Asculai, "How Iran Can Attain its Nuclear Capability—and Then Use It," in Ephraim Kam, ed., *Israel and a Nuclear Iran: Implications for Arms Control, Deterrence, and Defense* (Tel Aviv: Institute for National Security Studies, 2008), 13-32 (http://www.inss.org.il/upload/(FILE)1216205056.pdf).

7. For more on the nuclear issue, see Simon Shercliff's essay, which is chapter 4 of this book.

Prevention and Defense in Israeli Strategy

The failure of diplomacy and sanctions, to date, have revived Israeli discussion of the "Begin Doctrine," formulated in 1981 under Prime Minister Menachem Begin, when the government acted unilaterally to destroy the French-supplied Iraqi reactor in Osiraq after diplomatic efforts failed to result in international action. According to the Begin Doctrine, any state that acquires nuclear weapons and is actively involved in promoting violence and conflict would constitute an unacceptable threat.[8] (Pakistan is not considered to be a "confrontation state" and is not included in this category.) The Israeli raid that destroyed Syria's nuclear reactor in 2007 marked a second example of the Begin Doctrine and served as a reminder to Iran of Israeli policy and capabilities.[9]

In addition, there are unconfirmed media reports regarding discussions of options with the U.S. government.[10] On 13 August 2008, the deputy prime minister and defense minister, Ehud Barak, who also served as prime minister and Israel Defense Forces chief of staff, declared that "our position is that no option is to be taken off the table, but in the meantime, we have to make diplomatic progress."[11]

Prior to becoming Israel's prime minister in March 2009, Benjamin Netanyahu had compared the Iranian threat to that posed to Europe by Germany in 1938, declaring that "there is time to act in a variety of ways, and all ways must be considered, and all ways that work must be

---

8. *Haaretz*, 9 June 1981, cited in Shai Feldman, "The Bombing of Osiraq Revisited," *International Security* 7 (Fall 1982):114-43; Gerald M. Steinberg, "The Begin Doctrine and Deterrence," in *Israel in the Middle East—The Legacy of Menachem Begin.* Begin-Sadat (BESA) Colloquia on Strategy and Diplomacy 15. (Tel Aviv: BESA Center for Strategic Studies, 2000).

9. Editor's Note: On 6 September 2007, it is believed that the Israel Air Force performed an air strike on what some say was a Syrian nuclear reactor. For further reading on this event, see Ephraim Asculai, "Syria, the NPT, and the IAEA" (INSS Insight 53, Institute for National Security Studies, Tel Aviv, 29 April 2008; online at http://www.inss.org.il/research.php?cat=6&incat=&read=1778).

10. Aluf Benn, "U.S. Puts Brakes on Israel Plan to Hit Iran Nuclear Facilities," *Haaretz* (English edition), 13 August 2008 (http://www.haaretz.com/hasen/spages/1010938.html).

11. "U.S. Against Strike on Iran: Israeli Defence Minister," AFP Worldwide, 13 August 2008 (http://afp.google.com/article/ALeqM5hbHuCrDv8ufAXISj6SLUMFe_FxHw).

employed." He spoke of preemption, noting that "of all the activities required in the political, economic, and military fields, preemption is the most difficult. For us the Jewish people, too many times in our history we didn't see danger in time, and when we did, it was too late."[12]

At the same time, in considering a preventive military strike, Israelis are aware of the differences between the two previous implementations of the Begin Doctrine in the cases of Iraq and Syria. No single air attack would be able to destroy the multiple elements that constitute the Iranian nuclear program. The Iranians have learned from the Osiraq case and have dispersed, hidden, and hardened their nuclear facilities, making them far less vulnerable to attack.

However, the United States and Israel have also advanced significantly in terms of intelligence, targeting, and penetration in the past quarter century, including the development of precision long-range surface-to-surface missiles, reducing the need for vulnerable manned aircraft sorties. To destroy the fifteen to twenty key installations that are at the heart of Iran's nuclear weapons program, there would be no need for ground attacks and massive waves of airborne missiles aimed at Iranian military assets. Even if some facilities survive and others are well hidden and are not subject to attack, the large buildings housing the banks of centrifuges used for enrichment, as well as their very visible power supplies and related systems, and the foundations of the production reactor, could be damaged to the point that rebuilding would take many years.

Regarding the bellicose Iranian threats of retaliation, many of these are based on exaggerated military claims, including the use of photo-enhancement techniques and announcements of nonexistent exercises. Nevertheless, this is a factor in Israeli decision making.

---

12. Peter Hirschberg, "Netanyahu: It's 1938 and Iran is Germany; Ahmadinejad is Preparing Another Holocaust," *Haaretz*, 14 November 2006 (http://www.haaretz.com/hasen/spages/787766.html); for partial text of the speech, see "Netanyahu's '1938' Speech," Jewish Current Issues, 16 November 2006 (http://jpundit.typepad.com/jci/2006/11/netanyahus_1938.html).

Iranian capabilities include a small number of Shahab-3 missiles with a range of 1,300 kilometers, which could be equipped with chemical or biological agents, as well as Tehran's cooperative relationship with a dispersed and experienced terror network.[13]

In parallel, Israel has been accelerating its missile defense capabilities, including expansion of the operational Arrow system and research and development aimed at staying ahead of the Iranian ballistic missile deployment. As Israeli missile analyst Uzi Rubin has noted, "To date, the Arrow has scored fourteen successes in sixteen tests, a success rate of about 88 percent. . . . The system is currently in operation by the Air Defense Command of the Israel Air Force (IAF) in conjunction with the U.S. Patriot system, which serves as the lower tier in a combined two-tier missile defense array protecting most of Israel's homeland territory."[14] Israel has deployed three Arrow batteries, with eight launchers each holding six interceptors (a total of 144 Arrow interceptors). In addition, Israel deploys several Patriot PAC 2 batteries, to be upgraded to PAC 3 capabilities, providing the second tier for its missile shield.[15]

Deterrence and Its Limitations

Netanyahu's reference to 1938 and Nazi Germany reflects a widely held view in Israel that a nuclear-armed Iran ruled by fanatical leaders such as Ahmadinejad is incapable of maintaining a stable deterrence relationship.[16] This perception explains and is reinforced by the video clips of Ahmadinejad's statements, the scenes from the Holocaust denial conference, and the attention given to Iranian boasts of military "breakthroughs." From this perspective, Israelis reject the dominant

---

13. For a detailed analysis, see Patrick Clawson and Michael Eisenstadt, *The Last Resort: Consequences of Preventative Military Action against Iran*. Policy Focus 84. (Washington D.C.: Washington Institute for Near East Policy, 2008; online at http://www.washingtoninstitute.org/pubPDFs/PolicyFocus84.pdf).

14. Uzi Rubin, "Missile Defense and Israel's Deterrence against a Nuclear Iran," in Kam, *Israel and a Nuclear Iran*, 65-81 (http://www.inss.org.il/upload/(FILE) 1216205936.pdf).

15. Barbara Opall-Rome, "Israeli Defenses to Use Artificial Intelligence," *Defense News*, 21 January 2008 (http://www.defensenews.com/story.php?i=3361962&c=FEA&s=CVS).

16. Editor's Note: This perception is addressed by Mohsen M. Milani in his essay, which is chapter 5 of this book.

European position that the Iranian leaders are seeking nuclear weapons for deterrence, implying that Iran is a status quo power. Instead, the fanatical leadership is viewed as not subject to a rational deterrence relationship.

The attempt to apply the Cold War analogy of deterrence, based on assured second-strike capabilities and mutual assured destruction, to the Iranian leadership is very problematic in at least three important dimensions:

While the United States and Soviet Union were engaged in intense ideological confrontation, they had direct lines of communication, including diplomatic relations and embassies. This contact was extremely important in periods of instability that threatened the structure of deterrence. During the 1962 Cuban Missile Crisis, for example, the leaders were able to assess each other's intentions and commitment and to make decisions to de-escalate the conflict. Similarly, India and Pakistan have formal communications links, which served to de-escalate their crisis in 2000.

> 1. Iranian decision makers, in contrast, have no direct or indirect communication links with Israeli counterparts, increasing the likelihood of misperception and making crisis management extremely difficult.[17]

> 2. The very small size of Israel's territorial extent makes it difficult to maintain an assured and survivable second-strike capability, which is vital to stable deterrence. The narrowness of the Israeli borders and the ease with which they can be overrun by conventional forces, as well as the apparent vulnerability of a small number of bases to a first strike involving ballistic missiles, increases this perceived vulnerability. In contrast, Iran has a large territorial extent in which to disperse strategic weapons.

---

17. Gerald M. Steinberg, "Deterrence Instability: Hizballah's Fuse to Iran›s Bomb" (Jerusalem Viewpoints 539, Jerusalem Center for Public Affairs, April 2005; online at http://www.jcpa.org/jl/vp529.htm); Yair Evron, "An Israel-Iran Balance of Nuclear Deterrence: Seeds of Instability," in Kam, *Israel and a Nuclear Iran*, 47-63 (http://www.inss.org.il/upload/ (FILE)1216205527.pdf).

While Israel has reportedly addressed this issue by acquiring a small number of advanced diesel submarines, this is far from an ideal solution to the problem.

3. In a multipolar environment in which Egypt, Algeria, Turkey, Saudi Arabia, perhaps Syria (after the destruction of the North Korean-built reactor) and other Arab countries can be expected to follow the Iranian nuclear lead, stable deterrence is far more complex than the bipolar system of the Cold War.

In addition to the absence of direct communications between Israel and Iran, the lack of any form of significant contact is likely to create major misunderstandings and misconceptions, which could be extremely dangerous in a crisis. Leaders in Tehran and Jerusalem do not know how to assess the other's red lines and are not able to predict responses to various moves and countermoves. In this situation, there would be a strong likelihood of a spiral of destabilizing actions in which the decision makers respond to perceived threats through worst-case analyses without any history of interaction or expertise by which to interpret and predict further moves.

In the murky Iranian decision-making process, the power of elected and visible leaders and government officials is often secondary to the power of the clerics and the supreme leader, who operate in far greater secrecy, and whose understanding of the intricacies of stable deterrence is likely to be low. As a result, Israeli decision makers will have difficulty predicting Iranian policies and reactions. And while the Israeli decision-making process is far more public, and the governmental leaders are the key decision makers, the members of the Iranian inner circle appear to have no understanding of Israeli operational codes and responses to threat.[18]

The impact of such lack of contact and understanding was illustrated in the 2006 Lebanon war, in which Hezbollah leader Hassan

---

18. See Gerald M. Steinberg, "Parameters of Stable Deterrence in a Proliferated Middle East," *The Nonproliferation Review* 7 (Fall-Winter 2000): 43-60 (http://cns.miis.edu/npr/pdfs/73stein.pdf); Steinberg, "Walking the Tightrope: Israeli Options in Response to Iranian Nuclear Developments," in Judith S. Yaphe and Charles D. Lutes, *Reassessing the Implications of a Nuclear-Armed Iran.* McNair Paper 69. (Washington, D.C.: Institute for National Strategic Studies, National Defense University, 2005; online at http://www.ndu.edu/inss/mcnair/mcnair69/McNairPDF.pdf).

Nasrallah, who is closely linked to the Iranian leadership, admitted that he had totally misjudged the Israeli decision-making process and "disproportionate" response. Nasrallah said that he did not expect Israel to launch an all-out attack, including heavy bombing of South Beirut neighborhoods in which Hezbollah had strongholds, after the "limited" cross-border attack in July 2006 in which two soldiers were kidnapped (and later found to have died), eight others were killed, and the border area including houses and towns were subjected to heavy bombardment.

For Israelis, however, the need for a major response was clear, and there had been numerous public warnings to Hezbollah that were unheeded. For Israeli leaders, such kidnappings are unacceptable. They also saw a confrontation with Hezbollah as a means of demonstrating Israeli power and determination to the population and decision makers in Tehran and throughout Iran.[19] Hezbollah serves as an Iranian proxy force located on Israel's northern border, and Israelis saw this confrontation through this lens.[20]

Israeli Reliance on Washington and Its Limitations

Since the 1990s, when Israeli intelligence began to track accelerated Iranian efforts to acquire the technology for producing nuclear weapons, policy makers have maintained a low profile on this issue, emphasizing that the threat is global and needs to be addressed globally. In this post-Cold War period in which the United States was the uncontested superpower and global leader, this approach meant following the American lead and working closely with the U.S. in dealing with the Iranian nuclear threat. In 2003, after the initial phase of the second Iraqi War and U.S.-European tensions over Middle East policy, Israel reluctantly accepted U.S. President George W.

---

19. Ephraim Kam, "The Ayatollah, Hezbollah, and Hassan Nasrallah," *Strategic Assessment* 9 (August 2006; online at http://www.inss.org.il/publications.php?cat=25&incat=0&read=100).
20. Steinberg, "Deterrence Instability."

Bush administration's decision to agree to European leadership in the diplomatic efforts to contain Iran, despite recognition that the European Union policy was unlikely to slow or end the nuclear weapons program. Following the realization that this effort had failed, and as the United States again became the de facto global leader on this issue, including the sanctions process, the Israeli reliance on Washington returned to the previous level.

In November 2007, however, the publication of a short summary of the National Intelligence Estimate (NIE) on the Iranian nuclear program came as a major shock and shattered Israeli confidence in, and reliance on, American leadership. The summary, which was widely reported in the media around the world, claimed Iran had frozen its active efforts to manufacture nuclear weapons in 2003 and estimated that the Iranians would not have such a capability until at least 2012. This public document stated that the U.S. intelligence community had "high confidence" that the Iranians halted their nuclear weapons program in 2003, but only "moderate confidence" that Tehran had not restarted the program.[21]

Israeli intelligence analysts, as well as their British and French counterparts, had reached totally different conclusions. Israeli Defense Minister Barak stated in the wake of the NIE release that while it is "apparently true that in 2003, Iran stopped pursuing its military nuclear program for a certain period of time," he added that "in our estimation, since then it is apparently continuing with its program to produce a nuclear weapon."[22]

A number of factors can explain the differences in assessments. Israel, which would be the prime potential target for a nuclear Iran, cannot afford to take the chance of underestimating the threat. Therefore, it relies on what policy makers refer to as a "worst-case" analysis. This

---

21. Editor's Note: See National Intelligence Council, "Iran: Nuclear Intentions and Capabilities" (National Intelligence Estimate, November 2007; online at http://www.dni.gov/press_releases/20071203_release.pdf).

22. Steven Erlanger and Graham Bowley, "Israel Unconvinced Iran Has Dropped Nuclear Program," *New York Times*, 5 December 2007 (http://www.nytimes.com/2007/12/05/world/middleeast/05webreact.html?_r=1&scp=1&sq=Israel%20Unconvinced%20Iran%20Has%20Dropped%20Nuclear%20Program&st=cse).

means that the focus is on Iranian capabilities, rather than intentions, which can only be guessed. Using this approach, when Iran reaches the technological potential to produce enough fissile material necessary to make a nuclear weapon, it will be considered a nuclear state, capable of threatening Israel with annihilation.

Israeli analysts have warned their U.S. counterparts about the potential for a parallel "black" Iranian weapons program, based on a small nuclear reactor producing plutonium, following the North Korean model, as illustrated in Syria. Indeed, Iran is known to be constructing just such a reactor at Arak, leaving room for another undetected facility.[23] The consequences of a small, secret Iranian nuclear program are less significant for the United States, given its massive military superiority over Iran. Therefore, there is more room for political factors and influence in the official U.S. estimates.

The publication of the NIE summary and the headlines proclaiming that Iran had halted its nuclear program also had important political consequences and greatly reduced the ability of the United States to pressure and deter Iran through the threat of military force. Although President Bush responded to the NIE report by reconfirming his determination to prevent Iran from gaining nuclear weapons, Iranian policy makers most likely concluded that the probability of attack from the United States in the next five years had been rendered much less credible. Given the disquiet in America over the status of the situation in Iraq, and with an official assessment stating that Iran gave up its program to develop nuclear weapons four years ago, it was clear to all parties that the U.S. president would face strong opposition to any decision ordering U.S. forces into battle again. The fear of a potential Iranian counterattack, in the form of mass terror and possible missile attacks against American assets in the region, serves to increase this opposition.

The overall result of both the content of the NIE publication and the manner in which it was suddenly released, without any prior

---

23. Editor's Note: Arak is where Iran's heavy water reactor is located.

consultation, has weakened Israeli reliance on American security guarantees. As a result, a defense treaty designed to provide deterrence against eventual Iranian nuclear capabilities has become less credible in light of the NIE summary on the Iranian nuclear weapons program.

Conclusions

While Israel is clearly concerned about the potential impact of an Iranian nuclear weapons capability and has given this threat significant attention, in some ways, the discussions of this threat are part of the "normal" Israeli environment. New developments, including Iranian declarations regarding uranium enrichment, or missile tests, do not affect the Israeli stock market, for example.

Overall, the Iranian nuclear threat has reinforced the realism that forms the Israeli approach to security threats.[24] While there is still hope that international action, including serious sanctions, will stop Iran before the nuclear finish line, this is by no means assured. Proposals by foreign diplomats and academics suggesting that alliances such as North Atlantic Treaty Organization (NATO) membership for Israel could provide a sufficient response to an Iranian nuclear capability, or that a defense treaty with the United States would be important in this respect, are not likely to be seen as effective by Israelis. The U.S. is seen as weakened economically and overcommitted in Iraq and Afghanistan, and the weakness of European members of NATO, particularly with respect to security, reinforces the skepticism.

While there are many complexities, the possibility of a preventive Israeli military strike remains significant.

---

24. Gerald M. Steinberg, "Realism, Politics and Culture in Middle East Arms Control Negotiations," *International Negotiation* 10 (2005): 487-512.

Epilogue
The 2009 Iranian Presidential Election and its Implications

Karim Sadjadpour

Editor's Note: This piece was Karim Sadjadpour's written opening statement for his testimony before the U.S. House Committee on Foreign Affairs on 22 July 2009.[1] Sadjadpour kindly has allowed the reproduction of his testimony to provide insight into the post-election Iranian reality. His analysis offers perspective on how that reality has shifted the political landscape of the Iranian puzzle piece and on the impact that shift has on the potential for rapprochement with the United States. The one outlier in the evolving situation is whether there is time for the dust to settle within the Iranian political structure before the nuclear issue reasserts its position on center stage.

The enormous cloud of suspicion hanging over Mahmud Ahmadinejad's 12 June 2009 presidential election victory has produced the greatest political and popular eruptions in Iran since the 1979 revolution. Members of the committee have surely seen the remarkable images and amateur videos⊠ both heroic and harrowing⊠ that have emerged from Iran over the past five weeks.

The United States now faces a unique challenge. After 30 years of not having official relations, we finally prepared ourselves to recognize the legitimacy of an Iranian government, only to find that legitimacy has arguably been squandered. Now the administration of President Barack Obama has the difficult task of reconciling when and how to

---

1. A transcript and webcast of the full hearing on "Iran: Recent Developments and Implications for U.S. Policy" can be found online (http://foreignaffairs.house.gov/hearing_notice.asp?id=1101).

deal with a disgraced regime that presents urgent national security challenges, while at the same time not betraying a popularly driven movement whose success could have enormously positive implications for the United States.

I. Implications for Iran

The Regime's Eroded Legitimacy

The events of the last six weeks have had enormous implications for Iran. At a political level, the Islamic Republic of Iran has ceded any pretensions of being a republic. Past Iranian governments did not necessarily represent a wide swath of Iranian society, but they did encompass a fairly wide swath of the Iranian political elite. If the Ahmadinejad government maintains power, the country will be ruled by a small cartel of hard-line clerics and nouveau riche Islamic Republic Guard corpsman who reflect not only a relatively narrow swath of Iranian society, but also a narrow swath of the political elite.

Along with the legitimacy of the republic, another election casualty is the legitimacy of Iran's most powerful man, Supreme Leader Ayatollah Ali Khamenei. For two decades, Khamenei had carefully cultivated an image of a magnanimous guide who stays above the political fray, allowing him to deflect responsibility for Iran's deepening economic malaise and political and social repression. Those days are now over. In defiantly supporting Ahmadinejad, Khamenei has exposed himself as a petty partisan. Formerly sacred red lines have been crossed, as for the first time people have begun openly challenging Khamenei with chants of "*marg bar dictator*"—death to the dictator.

Despite the popular outcry, Khamenei has refused to cede any ground, believing that compromise projects weakness and invites more pressure. Today, his future rests largely in the hands of the regime's most elite fighting force, the 120,000-strong Islamic Revolution Guard Corps (IRGC). While growing fissures and dissent among senior clergy in Qom is certainly worrisome for Khamenei, dissent and fissures among top IRGC commanders would be fatal for him. While at the moment they seemingly remain loyal to him as their commander in chief, as the economic situation continues to deteriorate and popular outrage persists, their fidelity is not a given.

The Opposition's Plight

The popular implications have been equally enormous. At their peak, the demonstrations in Tehran included as many as 3 million people—according to Tehran mayor Mohammad Bagher Ghalibaf, himself a former senior IRGC commander—representing a diverse socio-economic swath of society, with women often at the forefront. While the scale of the demonstrations has subsided due to the regime's skilled use of repression, people's sense of injustice and outrage has not.

The more hard-line elements of the Basij militia seem to truly relish violence. People are up against an ostensibly religious government that has shown no moral compunction, a government that blames the murder of an innocent 26-year-old woman, Neda Agha-Soltan, on the BBC and CIA. Every time people take to the streets, they are risking their lives, and for every individual who takes to the streets, there are likely hundreds if not thousands more at home who feel solidarity with them. Nightly protest chants of *"Allahu Akbar"*—reminiscent of the 1979 revolution and meant to keep the momentum alive—have continued unabated.

The images and videos outside of Tehran have been similarly remarkable. In Isfahan, whose population is more traditional than that of Tehran, the demonstrators filled up the enormous Nagsh-e Jahan Square, the largest historic square in the world. Similar protests have taken place in important cities like Shiraz, Tabriz, Mashhad, and Kashan. In short, unrest has transcended age, religiosity, socio-economic status, gender, and geography.

One problem outside of Tehran, however, is that people are often less connected to the outside world via the Internet and satellite television, and have less access to technologies like video phones to document what is taking place. For this reason, there is much concern that the type of repression and human rights abuses that take place outside of the capital are much greater than that which has been documented only in Tehran alone. Outside of major cities, the regime's repressive apparatus can act with impunity and without accountability.

Nonetheless, the government's indiscriminate use of force and unwillingness to compromise have not forced the opposition into submission. Indeed, the current scale of repression has been both politically and financially costly for the regime. In the last week alone, former Presidents Hashemi Rafsanjani—a founding father of the 1979 revolution—and Mohammad Khatami have challenged the legitimacy of the election, with the normally timid Khatami even calling for a popular referendum. Grand Ayatollah Hossein-Ali Montazeri, the most senior cleric in Iran, recently issued a fatwa stating that the supreme leader is no longer fit to rule, arguably the greatest verbal challenge to Khamenei's leadership in the last 20 years.

The opposition's primary challenge at the moment is that its leadership and brain trust are either imprisoned, under house arrest, or unable to communicate freely. Despite the tremendous popular outrage, at the moment there is no leadership to channel that outrage politically.

Still, the financial costs of maintaining martial law, overflowing prisons, and media and communications blackouts are significant for the government. According to European diplomats, the Iranian government expends several thousand dollars per minute—tens of millions per week—to jam satellite television broadcasts from Voice of America and BBC Persian. Given the decline in oil prices, the current scale of repression will prove difficult to sustain for a long period.

II. Implications for U.S. Policy

Before President Obama's inauguration in January 2009, I wrote that "in charting a new strategy toward Tehran, the Obama administration must first probe a seemingly simple but fundamental question: Why does Iran behave the way it does? Is Iranian foreign policy rooted in an immutable ideological opposition to the United States, or is it a reaction to punitive U.S. policies? Could a diplomatic U.S. approach beget a more conciliatory Iranian response?"[2]

The Obama administration's unsuccessful attempts to change the tone and context of the long-fraught U.S.-Iran relationship, coupled with the events of the last six weeks, make it abundantly clear that Tehran's hard-line leadership—particularly Ayatollah Khamenei—views an adversarial U.S.-Iran relationship as politically expedient.

Whereas the George W. Bush administration unwittingly united Iran's disparate political factions against a common threat, the Obama administration's overtures accentuated the cleavages among Tehran's political elites. As one pragmatic conservative Iranian official noted to me several months ago, Tehran's hard-liners were under newfound pressure to justify their hostility towards the United States: "If Iran can't make nice with a U.S. president named Barack Hussein Obama who is preaching mutual respect on a weekly basis and sending us *Nowruz* greetings, it's pretty evident that the problem lies in Tehran, not Washington."

In light of the incredible events of the last six weeks, however, the Obama administration should reassess several aspects of its preelection policy toward Iran:

Don't Engage—Yet

When the demonstrations were at their peak, the Obama administration prudently refrained from inserting the United States into Iran's internal political battles for fear that we would taint those whom we aimed to help. We should continue to adhere to our policy of noninterference in Iran's internal affairs.

By prematurely engaging—before the dust has settled—we run the risk of implicitly endorsing an election that is still being hotly contested in Tehran and tipping the balance in favor of the hard-liners. This would

---

2. Karim Sadjadpour, "U.S. Engagement with Iran: A How-to Guide," *Middle East Bulletin*, 25 November 2008 (http://middleeastprogress.org/2008/11/us-engagement-with-iran-a-how-to-guide/).

demoralize the opposition and the millions of people who took to the streets and who continue to reject the legitimacy of the Ahmadinejad government. It is telling that one of the popular protest chants of recent weeks has been "Death to Russia," condemnation of Moscow's early decision to recognize the election results.

While the costs of engagement in the short term are very high, the benefits of immediate engagement are negligible. Tehran is still in disarray, and Iranian officials have not shown any indication that they are prepared or capable of making the types of compromises necessary to reach an accommodation with the U.S. when it comes to the nuclear issue or the Palestinian-Israeli conflict.

Engagement is not a policy in itself, but rather a tool that seeks, among other things, to curtail Iran's nuclear ambitions and moderate its regional policies. Premature engagement, however, could have precisely the opposite effect, by sending the signal to Tehran that its nuclear program is of such paramount importance to Washington that it can act with impunity. Iran would not be incentivized to limit its nuclear ambitions, but rather to expand them.

Pausing engagement until the dust has settled in Tehran does not mean renouncing it altogether. Given Iran's sizeable influence on several key U.S. foreign policy challenges—namely Afghanistan, Iraq, the Arab-Israeli conflict, nuclear proliferation, energy security, and terrorism—shunning Iran entirely is not a medium- or long-term option.

Don't Make Military Threats

If the events following the June elections proved one thing, it is that the Iranian regime is not suicidal. On the contrary, it ruthlessly clings to power and calibrates its actions accordingly. The Iranian regime, in other words, is odious but deterrable.

Indeed, the problem we have with Iran has far more to do with the character of the regime than the nuclear program. The reality is that as long as Khamenei, Ahmadinejad, and company are in power, we are never going to reach a modus vivendi which sufficiently allays our concerns—and Israel's—about Iran's regional and nuclear ambitions.

Based on both recent and historical precedent, there is good reason to believe that not only would Khamenei and Ahmadinejad not be cowed by military threats, but that they would actually welcome U.S. or Israel strikes in order to try and achieve the same outcome as Saddam Hussein's 1980 invasion of Iran—namely, to unite squabbling political factions against a common threat and keep agitated Iranian minds busy with foreign quarrels.

Ahmadinejad will also attempt to draw the United States into a war of words; we would be wise to ignore him. The Obama administration should continue to project the dignity and poise of a superpower rather than reciprocate the diatribes of an oppressive and undemocratic regime.

Condemn Human Rights Abuses and Help Ease the Communications Embargo

The Obama administration should not refrain from condemning the Iranian government's flagrant violence against its own citizenry and wrongful detention of political prisoners. While the regime claims only a few dozen have been killed and a few hundred imprisoned, European embassies in Tehran and independent human rights groups estimate that several thousand have been imprisoned and several hundred killed. Recent history has shown that outside pressure and condemnation works, as the regime incurs no costs for its egregious human rights abuses when the world remains silent.

One practical way of helping the cause of human rights in Iran is to help ease the communications embargo that Iranians are currently experiencing. Given the fact that foreign media were forced to leave and domestic media cannot freely report, everyday citizens bearing witness to events, whether via video phone or even simple e-mail or blog communication, have become very important. For this reason, the Iranian government has implemented Internet, satellite television, and SMS communication (text messaging) blackouts as a means of preventing Iranians from communicating with one another, and also with the outside world.

The United States and European governments, as well as NGOs and private-sector companies, should do everything in their power to ease this communications embargo. Companies like Siemens-Nokia, which have provided the Iranian government sophisticated technologies used for intelligence gathering and repression, should be publicly shamed and encouraged to donate their business profits from deals with Iran to human rights causes.

Don't Underestimate the Magnitude of this Moment

In an atmosphere of repression and intimidation, millions of Iranians throughout the country, representing a diverse swath of society, have taken to the streets since 12 June, agitating for greater political freedoms that many of us take for granted. Having endured a repressive religious autocracy for the last 30 years, Iran is arguably the only country in the Muslim Middle East in which popularly driven change is not of an Islamist, anti-American variety.

While the type of change Iranians seek may continue to prove elusive for months, if not years, we should not underestimate the size, strength, maturity, and resolve of this movement, nor its enormous implications. While this movement must be driven by Iranians themselves, it should remain a U.S. foreign policy imperative not to do anything to deter its success or alter its trajectory. Just as Iran's 1979 revolution dramatically impacted world affairs, so could the emergence of a more moderate, democratic Iranian government at peace with its neighbors and the outside world.

Glossary

Additional Protocol—The Additional Protocol is a legal document granting the International Atomic Energy Agency (IAEA) complementary inspection authority to verify all nuclear activities within a state that are provided in underlying safeguard agreements.

Assembly of Experts—*Majles-e Khobragan* is a group of eighty-six clerics directly elected by the people of Iran for eight-year terms. Considered one of the most powerful institutions in the Islamic Republic, the Assembly of Experts has the power to elect and review the performance of the supreme leader and technically can remove him from office. The Assembly of Experts candidates, similar to other elected officials in the Islamic Republic, have to be vetted by the Guardian Council, where the supreme leader has direct influence.

Ayatollah—Literally "Sign of God" in Arabic/Persian, it is the title for the high-level scholars among Shiites.

Basij—The term *basij* in Persian translates to "mobilization." In the Islamic Republic of Iran, the Basij, or Basij Volunteer Force (BVF), is the collective name for a volunteer public force formed by decree in November 1979 and accredited to the Islamic Revolution Guard Corps (IRGC). Officially there are more than 8 million BVF members who support the IRGC's mission of protecting the Islamic Revolution through various organizations, both military and civilian. Apart from the paramilitary and military organizations of the BVF, there are Basij organizations for teachers, artists, construction workers, etc.

Bazaari—From the Persian word *bazaar* (market), the Bazaari class refers to the Iranian merchant class.

Begin Doctrine—Israeli foreign policy by which Israel acts to prevent an enemy of the State of Israel from developing weapons of mass destruction. The policy is named for former Israeli Prime Minister

Menachem Begin (1977-83), who ordered the destruction of Iraq's Osiraq nuclear reactor in 1981.

Bushehr—City in Bushehr Province of Iran on the Persian Gulf coast. Location of the Bushehr nuclear power plant.

Dawa Party—Al-Dawa (The Call) is an Iraqi Shiite political party that was founded in 1958 and later opposed Saddam Hussein. The party forms a part of the Shiite Islamist bloc under the collective name of the United Iraqi Alliance. Although al-Dawa receives support from Iran, publicly the party supports *Wilayat al-Ummah* (authority of the people) as opposed to *Velayat-e Faqih* (authority of the jurists), the theory of government adopted by Iran after the Islamic Revolution of 1979 based on Ayatollah Ruhollah Khomeini's theories.

Expediency Council—Short name for the Expediency Discernment Council of the Regime (*Majma'-e Tashkhis-e Maslahat-e Nezam*), which was established in 1988 and now is a constitutional body meant to discern the interests of the Islamic Republic by trying to resolve cases of conflict between the Majles and the Guardian Council. Technically, the Expediency Council has the task of advising the supreme leader in strategic matters and can act as his unofficial deputies if he so elects. The supreme leader appoints thirty members of the Expediency Council and is also a member himself.

Guardian Council—Short name for the Guardian Council of the Constitution (*Shura'-ye Negahban-e Qanun-e Asasi*), which is a twelve-member council that approves all applicants for eligibility in Iranian elections and determines whether laws passed by the Majles are constitutional and based on the shari'ah (Islamic law). The supreme leader appoints six of Guardian Council members, and the other six are appointed by the Majles at the recommendation of the head of the judiciary.

Hamas—Islamic Resistance Movement, or *Harakat al-Muqawamat al-Islamiyyah*, is a Sunni Islamist Palestinian political and paramilitary organization founded in 1987. It has governed the Gaza Strip of the

Palestinian Territories since elected into power during the Palestinian parliamentary elections of January 2006.

Hejab—Arabic for cover or woman's veil. Refers to the Islamic dress code for women, especially the covering of the face.

HEU—Highly Enriched Uranium is uranium with the amount of uranium 235 isotopes (U-235) increased above 20 percent. A nuclear weapon requires enriched uranium with U-235 assays of 90 percent or more.

Hezbollah—Literally translated the "Party of God," Hezbollah is a Shiite Islamist political and paramilitary organization based in Lebanon. It was formed during the 1982 Israeli invasion of Lebanon. Since its inception, it has had strong ties to Iran. Its leaders were influenced by the Iranian revolution and declared Ayatollah Khomeini their leading religious authority. As a result of this relationship, Hezbollah has received ongoing support from Iran.

Hawzeh—The term is derived from the Arabic word *hauza* (area or territory) and refers to an area where mainly theological study takes place. The largest and most important of these centers in Iran is located in the city of Qom.

IAEA—International Atomic Energy Agency, based in Vienna, Austria, bills itself as "the world's center of cooperation in the nuclear field." Established in 1957 under the auspices of the United Nations, it works to promote safe, secure, and peaceful nuclear technologies.

IDF—Israel Defense Forces.

IRGC—Islamic Revolution Guard Corps, also known as Pasdaran (Guardians) from the organization's Persian name, *Sipah-e Pasdaran-e Inqelab-e Islami.* It was established in the wake of the 1979 Islamic Revolution in Iran with the task of protecting the newly established order from both foreign and domestic threats. The IRGC initially functioned as a safeguard against Iran's regular military, which was deemed as having loyalties to the ousted monarchal system. The

IRGC has its own ground, air, and naval forces in addition to the Basij and Qods Forces. Brigadier General Mohammad Ali (Aziz) Jafari has served as commander in chief of the IRGC since September 2007.

ISCI—Islamic Supreme Council of Iraq, which was known until May 2007 as the Supreme Council for the Islamic Revolution in Iraq (SCIRI). The ISCI is an Iraqi Shiite political party that was founded in 1982 and constitutes part of the "United Iraqi Alliance," a Shiite Islamist bloc. As an opposition group to Saddam Hussein, many of its leaders operated from Tehran until 2003 when Hussein was removed from power and they were able to return to Iraq. The ISCI continues to receive support from Iran.

LEU—Low Enriched Uranium is uranium with the amount of U-235 increased less than 20 percent. LEU can be used in civil nuclear reactors, which only require uranium that has assays of 2-5 percent U-235.

Majles—Short for *Majles-e Shrua-ye Islami* (Islamic Consultative Assembly), it is the Iranian parliament.

MEK—*Mojahedin-e Khalq*, or "People's Mojahedin of Iran" (PMOI), is a militant Islamist-Marxist political group. The MEK was founded in the 1960s and supported movements opposing the shah including the 1979 Iranian Revolution led by Ayatollah Ruhollah Khomeini. However, the MEK soon organized against the new Iranian theocracy, even supporting Saddam Hussein during the Iran-Iraq War (1980-88). The MEK operated with relative freedom within Iraq from 1986 until the U.S.-led invasion in 2003. After the invasion, allied forces confined the MEK to Camp Ashraf in Iraq, which has since been turned over to Iraqi control. The MEK's political wing is the National Council of Resistance of Iran (NCRI), and the group continues to be an active Iranian opposition group. Both the MEK and the NCRI are listed in the U.S. Department of State's "Country Reports on Terrorism 2008."

Natanz—Township in Isfahan Province where Iran's pilot fuel enrichment plant and its main commercial-scale fuel enrichment plant are located.

NIE—National Intelligence Estimate. NIEs are the Director of National Intelligence's (DNI) most authoritative written judgments concerning national security issues. They contain the coordinated judgments of the U.S. intelligence community regarding the likely course of future events.

Nowruz—Also spelled Navrooz, Nawrooz, or Nawruz, literally "new day." It marks the vernal equinox, which is the first day of the calendars used in Iran and Afghanistan. Celebrated as national holidays in Iran, Afghanistan, and some of the Central Asian republics, the holiday is particularly significant in Iran.

NPT—Treaty on the Non-proliferation of Nuclear Weapons, which entered force in 1970 and currently has 187 member states

Qods Forces—Literally meaning "Jerusalem" forces, this is a special unit of the IRGC that is active in organizing, training, equipping, financing, and supporting foreign Islamic revolutionary movements. The Qods forces are thought to facilitate and maintain contacts with underground Islamic militant organizations throughout the Islamic world. The group's perceived support and influence with organizations like Hamas and Hezbollah have aided in increasing Iran's regional influence.

Salafi—Derived from Arabic *al-salaf al-salih* (the righteous ancestors), this is a term that was originally given to an Islamic philosophical movement that began in the mid-19th century and advocated a return to the origins of Islam as a countermeasure to colonialism and the overall malaise of the Islamic world. In modern times, the term signifies those groups of Islamists who advocate a return to Islam's origins by changing the current state structures in the Muslim world through various means, including armed struggle and violence.

Sayyed (Seyyed/ Sayyid/ Said)—Derived from Arabic root *sada*—to be or become master, lord, or chief—the term *sayyed* in Arabic means master, sir, gentlemen, or is used as the honorific title for descendents of Mohammad. In the Iranian world, *sayyed* mostly refers to the descendents of Mohammad.

SCIRI—The Supreme Council for the Islamic Revolution in Iraq, known since May 2007 as the Islamic Supreme Council of Iraq (ISCI). See ISCI.

UF6—Uranium hexafluoride. UF6 is the compound used in the process of enriching uranium.

Velayat-e Faqih—"Authority of the Jurists," Ayatollah Khomeini's theory of Islamic government where the state is governed by a *faqih* (Islamic jurist).

Acknowledgments

This work is a compendium of essays that were presented on 17 September 2008 during a one-day symposium, "The Iranian Puzzle Piece: Understanding Iran in the Global Context," sponsored by Marine Corps University (MCU) and the Marine Corps University Foundation (MCUF) as part of the efforts of MCU's Middle East Studies. I wish to thank Major General Donald R. Gardner, USMC (Ret), under whose leadership as the president of MCU (2004-2009) the Middle East Studies was established.

Many other Marines and civilians from MCU also made contributions toward the organizing and execution of the symposium. In particular, a special note of gratitude is due to Dr. Jerre W. Wilson, vice president for academic affairs, for supervising the symposium from its infancy; to Dr. Kurt A. Sanftleben, vice president for instructional and research support, for providing the space and conference support; to Mary M. Lanzillotta for her tireless and patient handling of the contractual aspects; and to Bud Hilbmann and his team for making everything work.

The symposium was sponsored generously by MCUF from the beginning. Special gratitude is due to Brigadier General Thomas V. Draude, USMC (Ret), president and CEO of the foundation, and to John R. Hales, the COO.

The symposium and the current publication would have not been possible without the participation of the panelists, chairs, and those who enriched the session with their contributions in the form of questions and discussion. To the panel chairs, General Draude and Dr. Douglas E. Streusand, professor of international relations at MCU, thank you for making the symposium punctual and for guiding the question-and-answer period in a manner which made the entire day so much richer and more informative. I want to especially thank Professor F. Gregory Gause, director of the Middle East Program at the University of Vermont, for accepting the invitation to speak on Iran's policies in the Gulf region on short notice. General John P.

Abizaid, USA (Ret), opened the symposium, setting the tone for an excellent day of discussion on the Iranian piece of the puzzling world of the Middle East. I wish to thank him for accepting the invitation and for setting such a high standard for the rest of the day.

Many colleagues and friends provided suggestions for topics and speakers or facilitated meetings with the contributors. I wish to especially recognize Professor Wolfgang F. Danspeckgruber, director of the Liechtenstein Institute on Self-Determination at Princeton University, and Brigadier Phil Jones, military attaché, British Army Staff in the United States, for putting me in contact with several of the contributors to this volume and for their continued friendship and professional camaraderie. I extend thanks to Lieutenant Colonel Christopher C. Starling, USMC, for his help in arranging General Abizaid's participation.

To the contributors of this volume, thank you each and every one for accepting the invitation to speak at the symposium and for submitting your contributions. Your persistence through the stages of publication is much appreciated. While the symposium occurred close to a year before the publication of your contributions, I not only thank you for your collective patience, but also for your insightfulness, which has kept your writings relevant and forward looking. A special thank you to Karim Sadjadpour for granting permission to publish his congressional testimony on post-election Iran.

Kenneth H. Williams, senior editor of MCU Press, found the time in his demanding schedule to work on this volume. This publication would have not been possible without Mr. Williams' full support and efforts. Emily D. Funderburke of MCU Press, with assistance from Vincent J. Martinez and W. Stephen Hill, designed the book. Special thanks to Robin E. Joel for volunteering to design the symposium logo, schedule, and folder. The current cover is an inspiration of her work.

Erika A. Tarzi of the USMC Center for Advanced Operational Culture Learning read and edited the introduction and the final proof of the work and provided invaluable suggestions making it much fuller and finer. I am indebted to Erika for her efforts on this project and am eternally grateful for her companionship in walking this journey called life together with me.

Last, but certainly not least, I thank Michael C. Joel for working on every aspect of this project from the very beginning to the end. He was instrumental in organizing the symposium, worked—and often led—the publication process, and helped in the editing of the papers.

Contributors

Ali M. Ansari is professor of Iranian history and director of the Institute for Iranian Studies at the University of St. Andrews in Scotland, and associate fellow of the Middle East Programme, Royal Institute for International Affairs (Chatham House). He has authored numerous works, including *Iran Under Ahmadinejad: The Politics of Confrontation* (2007); *Confronting Iran: The Failure of American Foreign Policy and the Next Great Crisis in the Middle East* (2006); and *Modern Iran since 1921: The Pahlavis and After* (2003).

Mohsen M. Milani is professor of politics and chair of the Department of Government and International Affairs at the University of South Florida in Tampa. He is currently working on a book about Iran's regional policies.

Ronald E. Neumann is president of the American Academy of Diplomacy. Ambassador Neumann served previously as a deputy assistant secretary of state and three times as ambassador, to Algeria, Bahrain, and the Islamic Republic of Afghanistan. He was also the director of the Office of Northern Gulf Affairs (Iran and Iraq) as well as the principal officer in Tabriz, Iran. He is the author of *The Other War: Winning and Losing in Afghanistan* (2009).

Karim Sadjadpour is an associate at the Carnegie Endowment for International Peace. Previously, he served as the chief Iran analyst at the International Crisis Group, based in Tehran and Washington, D.C. He is author of *Reading Khamenei: The World View of Iran's Most Powerful Leader* (2008).

Simon Shercliff is the first secretary for counter proliferation at the Embassy of the United Kingdom, Washington, D.C. Previously he has served as a political officer in the British Embassy, Tehran; the chief press officer for the Foreign and Commonwealth Office; the first deputy director of communications; and the director of communications and press secretary for the foreign secretary.

Gerald M. Steinberg heads the Political Studies Department at Bar Ilan University in Ramat Gan, Israel, outside of Tel Aviv. He is the founder of the Program on Conflict Management and Negotiation at the university and is a fellow at the Jerusalem Center for Public Affairs. Some of his recent publications include "Examining Israel's NPT Exceptionality: 1998-2005" (2006); "The Centrality of Confidence Building Measures: Lessons from the Middle East" (2004); "Deterrence Instability: Hizballah's Fuse to Iran's Bomb" (2005); and "Israel at Sixty: Asymmetry, Vulnerability, and the Search for Security" (2008).

Amin Tarzi is director of Middle East Studies at Marine Corps University in Quantico, Virginia. He supports the university by providing a resident scholar with expertise in Iran, Afghanistan, Pakistan, and the Persian Gulf region. His latest work, *The Taliban and the Crisis in Afghanistan* (2008), is a coedited volume with Robert D. Crews of Stanford University.

Index

Index

www.ingramcontent.com/pod-product-compliance
Lightning Source LLC
Chambersburg PA
CBHW070116300326
41934CB00035B/1348